Mientje

Life's path is not made, but we make it when we start walking.

We do not know where it will take us but we can plan and hope.

The Girl Who Saw Too Much

Helmi Wolff

Helmi Wolff was born in Holland before World War Two, the youngest of seven children. She was educated there before moving to Oxford as an au pair in 1953 where she started her career in medicine as a specialised nurse. She later fulfilled her ambition as an artist.

She is married with three children. Her family encouraged her to write this book which is based on facts and real situations.

The Girl Who Saw Too Much

Helmi Wolff

Mientje aged two

The Girl Who Saw Too Much

Helmi Wolff

Mientje

May your home resound with happy sounds like good music.

To all those near or far, who helped in small or big ways and made our life more bearable and to all those we hopefully gave help and kindness in distress, never forgotten.

The Girl Who Saw Too Much

Helmi Wolff

The Girl Who Saw Too Much

Olympia Publishers
London

The Girl Who Saw Too Much

www.olympiapublishers.com
OLYMPIA PAPERBACK EDITION

Copyright © Helmi Wolff 2017

The right of Helmi Wolff to be identified as author of
this work has been asserted in accordance with sections 77 and 78 of the
Copyright, Designs and Patents Act 1988.

All Rights Reserved
No reproduction, copy or transmission of this publication
may be made without written permission.
No paragraph of this publication may be reproduced,
copied or transmitted save with the written permission of the publisher, or in
accordance with the provisions
of the Copyright Act 1956 (as amended).

Any person who commits any unauthorised act in relation to
this publication may be liable to criminal
prosecution and civil claims for damage.

A CIP catalogue record for this title is
available from the British Library.

ISBN: 978-1-78830-051-3

This is a work of fiction, but based on facts
as seen and interpreted by a little girl called Mientje.
Names, characters, places and incidents originate from the writer's
imagination. Any resemblance to actual persons,
living or dead, is purely coincidental.

First Published in 2014

Olympia Publishers
60 Cannon Street
London
EC4N 6NP

Printed in Great Britain

Helmi Wolff

*For my three children,
Carolyn, Michael and John.
With love and happy thoughts.*

Also in memory of so many unsung heroes to whom this book is dedicated with so much gratefulness and respect.

The Girl Who Saw Too Much

Helmi Wolff

Acknowledgements

With many thanks to my daughter, Carolyn, who encouraged me to write it down and get it published.

My son, Michael, who showed such grace and patience.

My son, John, for helping me all along with Computer knowledge and know how.

A big thank you to Del, for drawing the pictures to the chapters.

I wish to thank the Engine room in Bridgwater for their invaluable help in compiling dating and collating my manuscript at their drop in sessions and in particular I want to thank Will Bix for his constant help in completing my book.

Thank you Graham and Gloria for invaluable help with proof reading.

Thank you also to the memory of Di at 'Sunny Side Up' for allowing me access to their IT room
whenever I needed it.

Last but not least thank you to Bridgwater College
for helping me and printing the pages.

Not to be forgotten, Derek for his encouragement every day.

The Girl Who Saw Too Much

Helmi Wolff

Contents

Prologue	21
Introduction	26
Our Street (A)	28
Our Street (B)	34
My Earliest Memories	40
Seaside Outing	45
Escapade Down The Pear Tree	51
The Silver Wedding Anniversary	55
A Royal Ovation, Early 1939	64
Best Bib And Tucker	67
The Neighbours And Us, Knikkers!	75
Electricity In Our House	82
The Occupation	86
New Year's Day	96
Spring Cleaning	102
At Last, Big School	105
Bath Time And Small Bedrooms	111
Our Classroom	115
My Beautiful Pear Tree, Snakes And Nightingales	119
Another Washing Day	127

The Girl Who Saw Too Much

A New Grand Bathhouse	129
Play Nurses	133
Playing Shops 1942	136
Fun And Games (A)	140
Fun And Games (B)	142
The Windmill And Doggy Fun	145
Growing Veggies	151
Looking After Freddy	154
Lovely Freddy	159
Apples Under The Bed	161
Bad News	164
Blueberry Picking In The Woods	169
Lemele Berg	177
Liesje's Party	188
I Had Hardly Been Able To Concentrate On My Lessons All Day	191
Kite Flying And A Photograph	197
Piggy Pots, Rabbits And Cold Work	201
The Sergeant's Bike	205
A Story Mum Told	214
A Story Dad Told Us In All Its Glory	217
An Old Dutch Gin Bottle For Warmth	223
Traditional Dutch Midnight Christmas Dinner	227
Tiddlywinks	231
Goose Eggs	237

Helmi Wolff

Tienhoven	243
The Old Pram	245
Our Upside Down Bicycle	250
Tina	255
Beautiful Frost Stars	260
Our Last Six Weeks In The Little Cellar	268
The Liberation	273
Nightmares	277
The Dug Out	280
Homecoming	285
Analogue, On The 60th Anniversary – Commemoration of the Ill Fated	288

The Girl Who Saw Too Much

Helmi Wolff

What I observe is all part of human growth and development.

In acknowledgement and gratefulness to our liberators.
Without their brave and daring rescue,
we may not have lived to tell.

The Girl Who Saw Too Much

Helmi Wolff

Prologue

1939-1945 War experiences as seen through a child's eyes in the occupied country of Holland.

MIENTJE

A little, Dutch girl of four years at the start of World War II has her cosy life disturbed by the consequences of the invasion of Holland by the German army.

She could not yet realize the significance of how much her life would change. Her daddy and oldest brother, Rien, are taken by the Gestapo to be sent to Germany, to do hard labour, like clearing the rubble, the injured and dead, as well as working in factories.

She felt the pain as they were torn away from her mother's arms, and she cried with her mum. Missing them very much, she tried to write and draw to and for them, but as there was no address, her efforts never arrived.

Her mother was left to feed the family as best she could. The hardships that resulted were unimaginable. But through it all it was the steadfast optimism and sense of humour that sustained them.

Mientje's left foot was slightly bend inwards, which got her a lot of cruel teasing from the kids at school, as she had to wear her clumpy boots to straighten her foot instead of the wooden clogs everyone else wore. Consequently she was rubbish at sports and ball games, no matter how hard she tried. But she excelled at spinning tops and sweep; keeping it going all the way to school and back was no mean task on the sandy uneven roads.

Knikkeren involved rolling little coloured clay balls in a sandy pit to win the contents of the pot, and Hinkelen, a precision jumping game in a small measured space was another game she did enjoy.

Mientje's brother, Frans, was to become the mainstay as regards getting some food from the farmers, who were willing to help. Her sister, Hanny, also tried and helped, but was found a very good place in service with the ladies Moch, one of whom was the secret secretary to the palace, and from there Hanny was sometimes able to bring some food.

Mientje's friend's father had a windmill, and produced and processed many grains as well as livestock feed. The great mill stones could be heard softly grinding and pounding the corn and wheat and this was a comfort for many people. He was an essential part of the village for Apeldoorn's survival.

Vicky was Mientje's very young friend with whom she spent many hours of imaginative play. Her father was also taken from his family to work in Germany; they had a common bond.

The school was occupied during the last year by the soldiers, since the barracks had been bombed and destroyed, so the children had to take lessons at home. This involved meeting daily in the playground with the teachers, to collect their homework, which had to be returned the next day for marking.

Mientje's mother was born in Rotterdam; she knew the docks very well and was instrumental in helping many Jewish people get to the docks of Rotterdam, from where many made an escape mostly to America and England and Canada, in the submarines there. Even the family members of the 'House of Orange' had escaped that way, at the first signs of the war.

One day when Frans had gone with his friend, Gerard, to try and get some food and milk, the Deventer Bridge was targeted by a fleet of bomber planes.

This bridge is not so far from Apeldoorn, and the approaching drone of the planes could be heard and seen from Mientje's house.

The sky became dark at the far horizon, Mum who realized that the boys could just about be in that grave danger zone, sank down on her knees and prayed and prayed, calling out for help, to save her son and his friend.

The story they were told later is that they were actually cycling on the bridge, when they heard the ominous sound of the approaching fighter bomber planes. They threw their bikes over the bridge into the river, and dived in after them, to reach the relative safety of the other side. Then running for their lives, they ducked down at the nearest building they saw, shielding themselves by that wall, holding their hands tight over their ears and heads.

The bombing had started; the crashing and screaming of the falling explosives hitting all around them was deafening, causing bricks and concrete to fly high up in the air.

The bridge was not hit, but the factory was, and when afterwards they looked totally dazed around them, they saw that the wall at which they had been sheltering, was all that had been left standing intact, everything else was destroyed.

When they arrived at the top of the road to the homestead, Mientje spotted them, together on one bike, Frans peddling with Gerard on the back. They had even managed to recover one bike from the deep river.

A little girl of about eight years of age came: she had been walking for miles with a pram and her dead little brother inside. Something that Mientje saw, before her mother could intervene or help. It made a terrible impression on her.

It was Mientje's birthday; the promise of a picnic in Wilhelmina Park was dashed, as Frans came in visibly shaken, he told Mum not to let her out, as seven men had been shot, and their bodies displayed on street corners.

Mum tore the last remaining sheet into pieces, and went out together with their old Doctor Foster, to lay the white pieces of cotton over their faces. All Mientje could think when her Mum came home with red swollen eyes, was that something had happened to her daddy and brother, Rien, but she was reassured. She and her little friend, Vicky, were allowed to have their picnic in the back yard instead.

The Salvation Army played a part in their lives, by giving lovely, hot cups of soup or sweetish drink at the end of their service at which Mientje enjoyed the clapping for the choruses, and the lovely singing of the choir. Many a time they all linked arms with their neighbours, afterwards and clapped all the way home to keep warm and happy.

One of the happiest times for Mientje were the last six weeks before the liberation of Apeldoorn spent in a small cellar under the stairs, with her family of five. While the danger of bombing raged her mum tried to keep them happy by playing games and even being able to make a sort of chocolate drink made from roasted and grinded coconut shells left over from the matting factory.

One day a letter had got through from Dad. How elated they all were to hear that he and Rien were reasonably well. However this time it was terrible news.

Rien had had a small infection as a baby and because of that he was circumcised; this was spotted by the guards and consequently he was put into a concentration camp. The only way to get him out would be to get a Dutch birth certificate from Rotterdam town hall, which was destroyed by bombing. Mother left immediately to speak to a Rotterdam clergyman she knew. That man had saved the church stamps and seals from the wreckage, and was able to write a valid certificate stamped with the great seal of the church, to prove Rien's nationality.

Armed with this valuable piece of paper, Mum and the children camped, under some sheeting, near to 'no man's land', a strip between Germany and Holland. There they waited to see the next lorry driver who knew Dad, to give him that certificate of life. Rien was subsequently released after three months, but the dreadful experience scarred his life for good. Of course Mientje knew nothing of her mother's anguish, and the uncertainty that followed, about the safety of that one bit of important paper: to her, it was a happy little holiday, gambling about in the long grass as the weather was warm and little games were played to keep her occupied.

The ill-fated parachute drop, called: 'The Market Garden Drop', was witnessed by Mientje and Frans from the roof of their house. The sky was studded with parachutes, Mother called frantically for them to come down to safety, but they saw how the brave paratroopers were shot in the air.

Many of them killed or maimed badly. The survivors were marched along the roads of the village to the Juliana Hospital, some too injured to keep up, with hands folded behind their necks, still proudly wearing their purple/red berets.

Mum who was church organist, opened all the windows and doors of the house, to play and sing the English National Anthem on her piano loudly. Those poor souls heard it, and turned their heads that way, some even managed to smile.

Later that evening Mum crawled through the hedge of the hospital, where the soldiers were nursed in as many cots as possible. Mum had made many little comfort wishes on bits of card, from the Dutch people who were so grateful, which she gave to them.

She was caught, by the German commandant, but not all were completely insensitive, because he listened to her, when she asked him in her sweet manner: "If you were lying here injured or dying, do you not think, that your parents or wife or family would be helped, to know that someone was there to hold your hand, and speak words of comfort to you?"

The officer let her off, with a warning, not to do it again, but of course she did.

The Girl Who Saw Too Much

Introduction

At sixty years of age, I ventured back to Holland, having lived in England all my adult life, with my husband and three children, and all the other family who came to live quite near me too.

It was my daughter who encouraged me to write my life story, but more specifically, my memories about the Second World War as seen through the eyes of the little girl called Mientje.

I started telling some anecdotes to my grandchildren, and they listened to what we did and how we lived, the customs and way of every day quite simple life.

"Write it down, Mum," said my daughter, so I did. But as I had no experience in writing apart from letters, I wondered how to set about it, and maybe it would not only be for my family but others could be interested in the way a small child sees things.

Obviously it would not be an accurate recording of events and dates but, I felt that these eventful and varied stories should be recorded as remembered and felt by the little Dutch girl, who had her cosy life disturbed by the consequences of the invasion and occupation of Holland.

There were so many unsung heroes, thinking especially of my mother, who did so much for so many, and my father always ready to help anyone he could.

I was four years of age at the start of the war; my relationships with other young children, my brothers and sisters and the rest were evoked, and soon I found myself into the thick of those years.

I had a slightly deformed left foot, which pointed inwards more than usual, so I was therefore unable to compete in running and ball games, which caused me a lot of upset, also bullying and teasing from other children.

I recalled the horrific episodes of war that concerned us directly, including escapes by a whisker from dangerous situations, heartbreaks and hardships, all as seen and felt by Mientje, also the fun times and childish pursuits during my school years.

Wonderful memories popped up, such as our pear tree in full blossom, appearing to me like the frothy lace of a bride's dress and veil I'd seen in a picture.

Or the beautiful sunset I saw from the flat roof over our patio, even if it scared me a little, as I imagined an angel in the middle of the fiery clouds.

Also an early outing in my father's car to the seaside, when I was only three and half years old, made a huge happy impression on me. Later when horrible things started to happen I was able to recall this and hide behind these happy memories.

One of the best times for me during the war, were the last six weeks living in our very small cellar with my family. In the midst of bombers flying overhead, Mum with all her cheery inventiveness made the experience fun and with a feeling of being safe there. The amount of laughter and banter coming from us, being so pushed for space to lie down, was amazing.

But it is only now that I realize how worried Mum must have been for our safety. She just battled on with great fortitude and determination, that saving attitude she had adopted since the day my dad and my eldest brother had been taken by the Gestapo.

The Girl Who Saw Too Much

Our Street (A)

When I visited Apeldoorn for the first time in many years, I was pleased to see that the tiny village had blossomed into a bustling town. Of course the sand roads had all been tarmacked now, with the smallest of pavements on either side for walking and cycling, which is still very popular.

Our house was still standing and seemed so much smaller than I remember it. How did we all fit in at the time? I hesitated when I walked up to the old house. Was that all it was, a typical square construction with a pitched roof and chimney? I could see the front bedroom windows through which we picked horse chestnut leaves for play, now painted green and neatly curtained. I can't remember us ever painting anything. I think the woodwork was grey in our day.

Helmi Wolff

The downstairs of our house and garden.

The Girl Who Saw Too Much

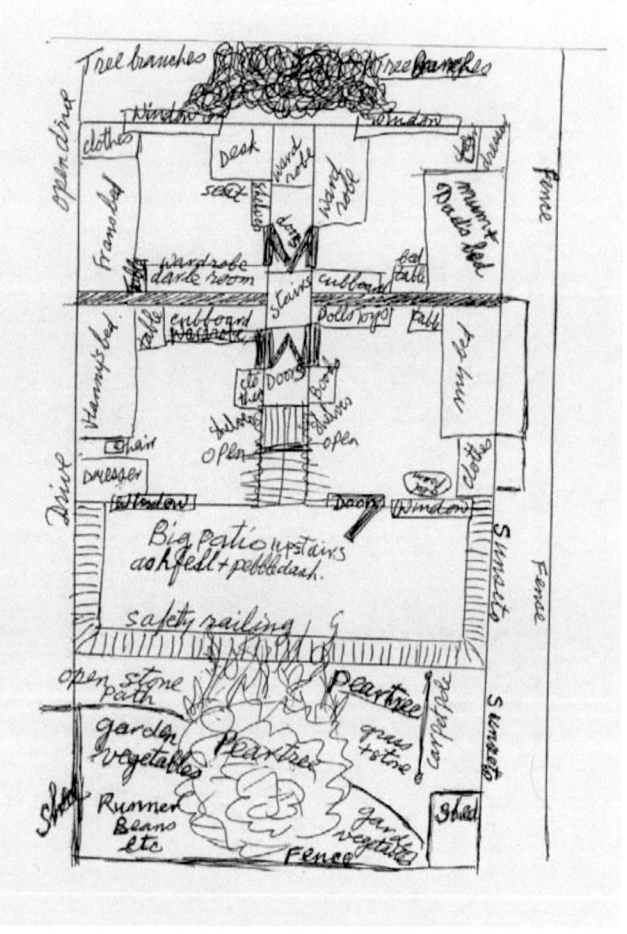

Upstairs under the eaves.

I wondered if anyone I knew still lived in the area. I guess not our neighbour, the painter and decorator Mr Barrevink, who had been very ill with lead poisoning, and was given a special allocation of milk to counteract the zinc and lead residues in his blood, but he was often known to sell or exchange the milk for other food.

As I stood there thinking, a very old lady came walking out of her house opposite. She looked at me intently and asked in her broad Apeldoorn accent, "Can ioye elp yer me deuire?" I turned around and instantly recognised the dear old face of Mrs Backer. She must have been ninety-six years old by now. "Mrs Backer?" I asked.

"Dus I noo yer?" I smiled to myself, as her accent was still the same!

"It's Mientje Wolff, Mrs Backer." An incredible look spread over her lovely old face and a sparkle of recognition lit up her keen blue eyes.

"Oh my: Mientjen mit de 'vlechies'!" Meaning, Mientje with her hair in two braids, as I always wore it as a child. I said it was wonderful to see her, and that I did not expect to see anybody I knew after so many years. Mrs Backer welcomed me into her house, through the same old back door I knew so well. Overcome with pleasure at the surprise of seeing me again, Mrs Backer asked, "How are you, me child?" at which we both burst out laughing as I was now sixty years old!

A coughing fit shook her small, frail frame and it took some time for her to recover.

I stretched my arms around her to hold her up. Nothing much had changed indoors. The furniture was still very sparse and functional. The fireplace had been replaced with central heating.

In the kitchen she busied herself making a cuppa for three. She explained that the third drink was for Theo who was upstairs. When

I enquired who that was, she said, "Mr Backer." Obviously as a child I never found out the Christian names of adults. A faint memory conjured up Mr Backer as I remembered him, chewing tobacco and singing little songs for me. He must have been even older than her. He had never seemed fit all those years ago and he walked with a stoop. Mother said he was born like that.

I remembered when I was four years old being sent across to the Backer household with a cup to ask for some sugar. "I've got something for you, Mientje," he had said. Keenly I approached him. "But first," he said, "we have a song." It was a silly little ditty, which amounted to:

'Mientje Katrientje zit achter het gordientje
wat deed ze daar
ze kamde haar haar
ze poetste haar tantjes
ze waste haar handjes
in haar zij alleby
zo varen de scheepjes voorby.'

In English,

'Mientje Katrientje sat behind the curtain
What was she doing there?
She was combing her hair
She was washing her hands and brushing her teeth
Hands in her waist
And so the ships sail away.'

Anxiously looking forward to what he had for me, I eagerly responded to his request of, "Stretch out your hand and close your eyes," whereupon he slapped something warm into the palm of my little hand. "Open your eyes," he instructed. How horrible, he had spat out his chewed tobacco and deposited it into my hand. I shook it off me and mumbled some audible "Oohh ughh" whereupon Mrs Backer came in to see what the consternation was about.

A severe telling off followed from her to him and Mr Backer never repeated that filthy episode with me. The filled cup of sugar made up for the experience and Mum was pleased with it.

The Girl Who Saw Too Much

Our Street (B)

The rag and bone man came through Bartelsweg (road) calling loudly "Rags and bones," whilst ringing his huge bell. I never quite knew what he could do with old bones but I liked to see the horse and cart coming through. Sometimes the horse had a nosebag hanging from his head with some tasty morsels in it. You could hear the strong munching and crunching of the huge jaws sliding over each other. If you came fairly close, the musty smell of his breath would almost knock you over.

The milkman was next. Old Jo Smienk had a pushcart upon which stood four big milk churns. He pushed the heavy vehicle through our road, past our house, all the way from his farm with the fresh milk straight from the cows: no pasteurisation then. Ringing a gleaming brass bell furiously, he'd stop at strategic points to sell his milk.

All the housewives came out to fill their milk pans, which were tall, enamelled pans with a fluted hole in the middle of the lid and five smaller surrounding ones to prevent the milk from boiling over.

"Out of the way, Mientje, your mum will get her turn," was often said, as I was there first. Ah, but I was hoping for a lick of lovely rich milk when it dripped from the outside of the pan. Jo had two measuring ladles, one of a quarter and another a half litre in size. They hung on long handles inside the churns. He lifted them out carefully to fill each pan, avoiding wastage. Jo also played in the brass band of the Salvation Army and we sometimes went to hear them during the week.

My brother, Frans, had already learned to play the cornet there, and Hanny had joined the choir. She was given a uniform and pretty hat to wear.

I couldn't wait to join and get a lovely bonnet and jacket like that, to wear as well.

The baker, Kees Buisman, had a tricart, which was like a tricycle with a large box on top and opening doors. Inside was the warm freshly baked bread. He hardly needed to ring his bell as the gorgeous smell could be detected from the top of the road and everyone came running out to buy, at the merest ring.

He was a very little man in stature but had a booming voice. "Brood voor alleman," (bread for everybody) he would shout and he really had lots of it.

"See you later," Piet Kaaskop would shout a few doors up from ours. I didn't know it then, but Piet and Kees worked together, baking the bread in the early hours of the morning with long paddles in a very hot oven.

Jopie, the vegetable man, came along three times a week with his luscious fruit and vegetables, pushing his cart whilst shouting for custom. His orange carrots were proudly displayed on the top. Now this was a forbidden colour to wear, have, or show in any way during the war years as it was the national colour of the Dutch Royal family, 'The House of Orange', who had all escaped to England by then. But still the cart was covered with orange carrots. He was quite a daring young man as this was a defiant thing to do.

One fruit that was quite rare was the tomato. It was reported to be the fruit of good health and youth. During his banter one day, to mostly appreciative and impressionable young housewives, Winking and blinking, he stretched to his full height, and pushing out his muscular chest, he told them, "Not to forget to give some to your husbands too!" To which some giggling and sniggering could be heard from the girls.

At that point, two German soldiers came marching along the road. They spotted the crowd of women and the showy young lad at the centre of attention. They then eyed the totally orange cart festooned with perky carrots. Fury overtook them.

Pushing and shoving and shouting abuse, they punched young Jopie down and turned over his cart, sending all his wares sprawling and rolling down the sandy road.

The women ran, some taking with them what they could scoop. Jopie, however, was never seen again after he was marched off to the German barracks to be interrogated.

Jopie's elderly father, who grew most of the vegetables, was in a field down the next road, he must have heard the commotion, and came running to the spot as best he could and, with some help, pulled up the cart, carrots and all. When later he was asked what happened to his son, he would just say, "Gone, all gone," with great despondency.

Helmi Wolff

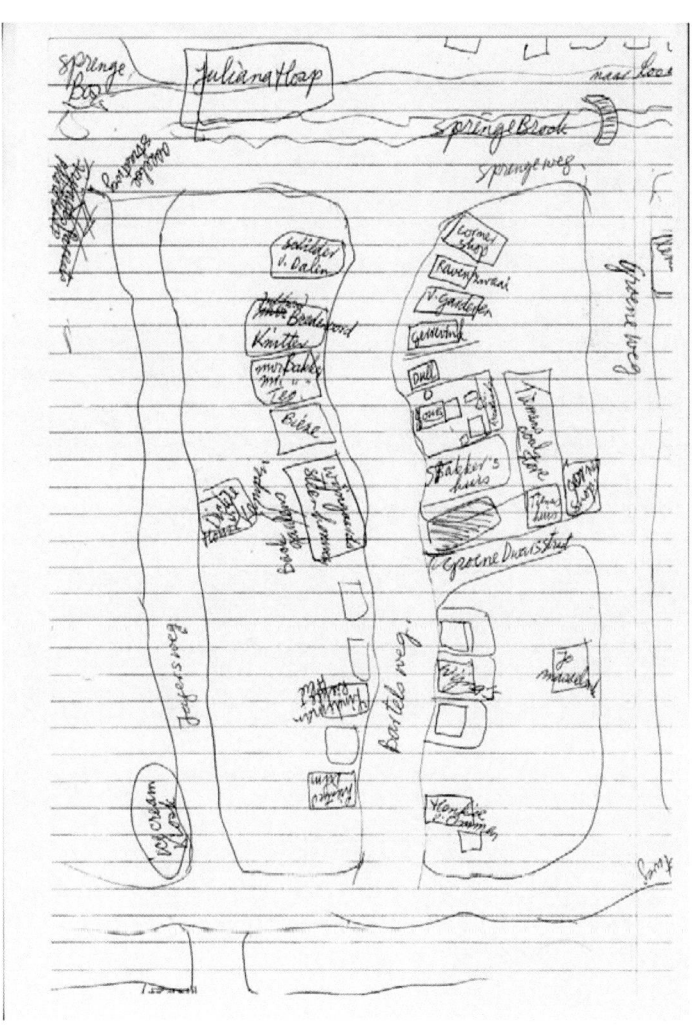

Our street and the neighbourhood.

The Girl Who Saw Too Much

Our village.

Helmi Wolff

All our family and Aunt Marie's family at the play garden of 'Juliana Toren' (Tower).

The Girl Who Saw Too Much

My Earliest Memories

I think my very earliest memory must be an impression really, but one which I can nevertheless conjure up. I see a vague hue of blue and hear a crash. Apparently I was a late walker (due to problems with my left foot) and still quite tumbly at two and a half years of age.

I had crawled or waddled under the round table in the dining room. Mother was expecting guests, and had laid the table with the best china on a blue flowery tablecloth. I looked up, saw something beautifully blue and decided to pull myself up by it.

Well, *crash bang, boo hoo*! Sometimes I still see that hue of blue if I concentrate, but whether it is a real memory of the crash, or an ingrained abhorrence of sudden loud noises or bangs, I don't know.

Another fond early memory I have is of my lovely blue pushchair. Dad had made it from bits of triplex wood, which was quite a new thing then. It was strong, thin and light. I remember it so well, even though I can't have been older than three and a half years of age. The seat was reinforced with thicker wood and had lovely carved arms and hand rests, it also had a long T-piece on the front to push or pull.

Two little wheels were attached underneath and the whole thing was painted blue, with a white daisy on both outer sides.

For luxury and comfort, mother's cornflower blue skirt was cut up to make a long cushion attached to the back. I was taken to see it one morning after Father had been secretly busy in the shed. It might have been an early birthday present. I fell in love with it at first sight, and adored being taken on outings in it.

I certainly remember the pre-pushchair days when Mum and Dad used to carry me in a canvas seat with wooden handles.

Even before that, I remember how they used to link fingers underneath and behind me for support during long walks as my foot became tired.

Of course later, special high boots were made for me, to help correct the way I walked.

I was unable to wear the traditional wooden clogs, due to harshly kicking my right ankle with the poorly left foot.

I was also extremely prone to falling on my knees, and spraining my ankles and wrists.

My dad used to clean the scrapes, rub butter into the wounds, bandaging them with long wet strips of torn sheeting soaked in vinegar.

Another great occasion was going to the local waterfalls at Loenen. These were man-made steps dug out and concreted to create seven or eight broad but short falls. This was the start of the Sprenge Beek (Spring Brook), which flowed at the top of our road. It was an extra special Sunday outing in Dad's wonderful old car with Hanny, Frans and I.

Once, after Mum produced the customary picnic of sandwiches and lemonade, we went to paddle in the stream and climb up the waterfall, which was very hard to do as it was slippery and the water coming towards us was quite violent to me. Han and Frans dragged me up like I was a rag doll.

I remember facing a wall of water but I knew they would look after me, and we'd get through to the other side. Once we had actually reached the top, they held me aloft shouting to Mum and Dad to look.

Suddenly I saw Mum looking terrified and racing at the side of the fall towards us. The next thing I knew was that I was taken down to stay with them.

Frans found some edible wild chanterelle fungi. They are shaped like beautiful curly yellow combs, quite large and tasty. Mum was delighted and we ate them the next day. However, we wanted to find more and wandered into the surrounding woods quite a long way.

Suddenly a thudding roar startled us, and a herd of wild swine raced by. I can only see this in my mind's eye but Frans told us to stay still, all three of us did not move a muscle. He was so knowledgeable about so many things. I think he learned much practical know-how in the boy scouts, which he stayed in all through his schooling. Eventually he became a scoutmaster of a very smart team, winning small and large awards, and I think this had a great influence on him later in his musical career as a bandmaster and brass band virtuoso.

Meal times were something else. The thick tapestry tablecloth came off, and the dinner table was laid out, on the bare scrubbed wood. Mother brought in the dish with *'boeren kool'* and worst, (curly kale and potatoes pounded together) and a thick meaty sausage: or *'zurekool met spek'*, a 'sauerkraut' and potatoes mixture with bacon all cooked together, or brown beans and onions, 'stamp-pot'. When she finally put it on the table, we all folded our hands in thanksgiving.

Sometimes I could not resist peeking, to see if everyone had closed their eyes. Once I saw Hanny peeking too, and we nearly had a laughing fit but just managed to stay serious until the prayer of thanks was over.

I hated red cabbage, so Mum stirred in a little of Dad's brood pap (bread soaked in sugary milk), to disguise the dreaded taste. It got a bit tedious sometimes, and I had a habit of rocking my chair on two legs, at which Dad would say, "A chair has four legs Mientje."

"Oh yes!"

Helmi Wolff

The Girl Who Saw Too Much

Freddy was always hovering under the table, which was handy for me in quickly passing the bits of red cabbage to him. That dog was so switched on to see where a hand came down with something for him in our fist, but he did not like red cabbage either, however, he made a pretence of swallowing it. The trouble was that it always made him sneeze – what a give away!

Father's first mobile exhibiting vehicle used to advertise the latest soap powder etc. He and his friend Jan Bensink towed it to street corners and village centres, to show how clean the washing in the vehicle was with Klok-Zeep (sunlight soap). He had a wind up gramophone, playing music to attract people and show them the goods.

Helmi Wolff

Seaside Outing

"Oh no," said Mum, "not another old banger please," as she could hear some clanking and exhaust banging, coming down the road. She looked out, and saw Dad in this huge old black car.

He was red in the face with the efforts of driving it home, and into our broad gravel drive, which Rien and Dad had prepared all week, and in doing so they had taken half of Mum's garden, with the hydrangeas and gladies.

They also removed the end wall of the wooden shed, to hang a big straw matting curtain there instead, to be able to work on the jalopy in the dry if it rained.

All a bit of a mystery to me, but I bet Mum had an idea.

Anyway here was the object of the exercise, a gleaming big monster of a car parked in the space. Mum looked at it whilst laughing, she had hoped for a sleek silent limousine.

"Oh man. Why is this one so noisy?" Mum asked. "I had dreams of a nice quiet car in soft blue."

"Come and see the inside," Dad ventured, "all real leather you know, and plenty of room for all of them."

He opened the folding bonnet, and started up the engine with the crank handle again, Mum was off like a shot. "I'll never get used to that racket," she said, whilst she stood, sort of protected in the doorway.

Dad put his head inside the bonnet, prodding about a bit and said, "It's a good car you know, lass, the auctioneer said so!" Standing close by, I was suddenly lifted up to see the inside. Oeee! Lots of funny seats and what is that stick for. I explored the inside of this new thing like a wondrous cavern. Dad came to sit in the driver's seat and put me on his lap, with my podgy little hands on the steering wheel, making funny noises like, "Brr, brrrrrrr, brrroom, broom."

I took to it like a fish to water, and would not come out. "I want to play with my dolls in here, it is a house on wheels," I squealed.

A lot of work was done on the car before it was ready for the long awaited holiday to the seaside, and also to go and visit Aunty Ans and Uncle Koert in Scheveningen, a long way from Apeldoorn.

The day arrived and it looked promising, everyone was so excited, as Dad proudly backed out of our drive with all of us inside.

I sat on Nelly's knees and felt so safe and cosy, with Hanny and Frans either side of us in the back of the 'wonderful house on wheels'. Mum and Dad had loaded lots of things for our survival into a big box which was strapped onto the boot and another also, onto the side running-board.

I don't remember the entire journey but we had several stops and small picnics on the way, owing partly to the fact that Dad had to repair seven punctures, plus the engine had to cool down every ten kilometres, and the steaming radiator topped up with water from the big tank strapped to the other side runway. Every time I saw the steam rising in front of us, I thought Mum was making tea that often, and in the meantime we had lots of fun too!

Mum laid out a blanket on the grass verge, to stretch her legs. I knew it was picnic time again. We all scrambled down but I was put into my blue wooden pushchair, as there were now other cars on the roads. They took me in the woods and we played 'Hide and 'Seek' and also 'Boom Verwisseltje', (a game of running from tree to tree without getting stopped by the person in the middle). Nelly, Hanny and Frans decided to hide from me, but I could hear their giggling behind the trees.

I had to concentrate on where to run on my little four-year-old legs with the silly left foot. It was a bit scary in case I'd lose them, but it was absolutely hilarious when I saw them. "I caught you all!" I screamed!

The rest of the journey is a bit vague as I started to get uncomfortable, and began wriggling. "Sit still," Nelly said.

"But you've got bony knees," I replied. She looked at me and passed me onto Hanny. I soon fell asleep.

We did eventually see the sea, it was the first time for me and it looked so big.

"Where does all that water come from, Mum? And who put all that sand there?"

After a while of sheer awe, they all started paddling in the shallow froth and the first shallow waves on the beach of Scheveningen. Mum had made swimsuits for all of us, mostly from old jumpers, cleverly cut and sewn; the hems were done in bright yellow buttonhole stitch. I had noticed that she never wore the same colour cardigan that a neighbour had knitted for her. Ahhhhh a light went up for me!

Tentatively I also put my toes in so much water I was a bit worried but soon I was paddling with them. Frans sprinkled more wet on me and Hanny joined in gushing me with the brine. Screaming did not help, so I tried doing the same, only to slip and get completely christened. Both my hands were gripped and they hauled me up right into the air, aha! I can do that, we played and laughed and ducked one another. The fun was enormous, but the wet swimsuits by now had sagged, with the crotch hanging down to our knees.

We arrived at Aunty Ans and Koert's at dusk. It was past my bedtime. I only noticed that she looked so kind, but very old. She took me from Hanny saying, "Ohhh, so this is our Mientje," setting me on her lap which was very big and her long green apron only just met around her. "Oh," she said again, "haven't you grown, love? Would you like a cookie?"

"Oh yes please, Aunty."

We ate a lot of the meal they had prepared for us and slept on mattresses on the floor but we were much too tired to care. Mum said, "It is very good of you both to put us all up for the night." My Aunt just smiled and said she loved us all. Uncle Koert was very quiet but helped us all to get comfortable.

The next day we all went to the sea together. Uncle Koert bought an ice cream for us all. We had not seen such a sort of drink in a cone before, but it tasted lovely. The yellow sand dunes seemed to stretch before us as far as the eye could see.

It was a lot to take in for us, especially me. And when I was taken into the sea in my still damp swimsuit I screamed again with excitement as the cold water flowed over my waist, but this time they said, "You must learn to swim!" I soon found out what that meant, when the tide sent an extra big wave, Frans was holding me, but the salt water got into my mouth and I panicked.

Shivering and shaking I was thankful to be on dry land again. Mum said, "Cuddle up we'll have a little snooze." When I woke up I saw that they had been building a sandcastle. But I didn't know that and blurted out, "What is that growing next to us?" They had decorated the castle with lovely shells, and all around a ditch, which they called a moat, which later on filled with water to wash the whole structure away.

We saved the shells, and Nelly took me to find a lot more, some like angel's wings, in soft pink and lightest yellow. Others had a lovely rainbow sheen which was **paarlemoer**, (mother of pearl). There were others like little fans in mottled brown or grey, but the ones I liked best were the crinkly shells in which a little creature had lived in the sea. Nelly explained that the little sort of fish had swum away but the sea had washed its little house up on the shoreline.

We gathered others too, like small clams and Frans found a starfish, but Dad told him to throw it back into the sea. I was sorry to see it go as it was absolutely gorgeous. These shells were taken back home and kept. Hanny showed me how to glue them onto a paper sheet like a collage, which was hung on the wall, but because some of them dropped off, I covered them up and kept this treasure under the bed to bring out now and again to see and show to friends and neighbours.

I don't recall the way back from the holiday, but I woke up in my own little bed a few days later.

In my pushchair at the seaside.

The Girl Who Saw Too Much

Dad's wonderful old Ford with Gran and us.

Helmi Wolff

Escapade Down the Pear Tree

My twenty-year-old brother Rien was still at home, but off and on depending on the job he had.

When my Mum and Dad moved from Rotterdam to Apeldoorn with their brood, it was to make a home in their own house.

They were met at the station by my grandfather, Vaatje Goudkuil, who was waiting with his wheelbarrow to help. He took one look at my mother who was heavily pregnant and said, "You'll be best off in the wheelbarrow, lass." The rest of them trudged behind. Soon afterwards Hanny was born, then Frans and six years later I was born.

"Go get the midwife, Hanny," Mum said, which was easier said than done.

"I think she's lost her way."

"Go see after her, Frans." They came back panting.

"She's on her way, Mum… Oh she's here!"

"Too late," Mum said.

Was it the way she grabbed me in her haste and held me upside down by my feet and smacked my little bottie that did slightly deform my left foot? "We'll never know now," Mum said. "You were quick then and you've been quick ever since."

Father's mother had already moved there, as she believed that we would have a second world war not long after the 1914–18 one, in which Dad served.

She knew a small time builder in Apeldoorn, and as she had saved all her life, was able to buy a new house from Mr Stakker in the Bartelsweg; she also secured a second place for us right next door to her, and on the other side was Mr Stakker's own place.

Mr Stakker was a big red-faced man, who kept himself to himself and did not have time for children, but he was interested in taking Rien on as an apprentice carpenter. Rien needed to earn his keep so he started work there.

He quickly learned to operate the electric saw, which we could hear whirring all day. Mrs Stacker was more approachable, and sometimes I picked a little bunch of field flowers for her with which she was always pleased. She would invite me in to give me a sweet or even a drink of lemonade. I once asked her if there were any children to play with, but she looked sad and just said, "No," and I knew not to ask any more questions, although I could hardly imagine a home without children.

It worked out very handy for my dad being able to borrow tools or buy materials for building an extension at the back of the house including a large semi closed-in patio, with a strong enough roof over it to support an upstairs sort of garden, properly fenced in, for us children to play in and also for Mum to hang the washing. Access was via a new door leading from the two small bedrooms adjoining it.

This is where I stood so many times looking at the beautiful sunsets and being a little afraid of the glorious colours, as in the middle I imagined an angel, coming down to speak. As I had been told by my very strict teacher that if I was naughty I would be punished, and would never be allowed to go to heaven, that scared me, but mostly I played there with my little friend, Vickie.

The pear tree was within reach as it hung over the upstairs patio, which meant that we could pick the lovely juicy pears from there when ripe.

Mum sometimes went out in the evening to her various church clubs; it was then that Rien could practise his accordion. He learned to play by ear, and he had perfect pitch, singing the lovely romantic songs he liked. I would have been tucked up in bed already, but often if I heard the music I'd slip out and down the stairs, in my flannelette nightie to listen to him.

"Are you going to dance for me then, Mien?"

"Yes," I replied and promptly started to sway and whirl to the rhythm of the song, prancing round and round the little backroom. On and on he played and sang. I was quite swept away with the music, jumping on and off the chairs and table all in a fantasy of movement and dreamy sounds, until I'd tire and was brought back to bed. I was a little in awe of my big brother but he was always kind to me.

He was quite a lad about town, and so good looking. I loved to see him dressed to go out in his Sunday best, and on this particular night it was his tie, which gave him trouble, He was going to meet some girls with friends in the village and the tie would not do as told. I could hear him mumble and tug at the blessed thing but nothing helped. Rien was known to have a short fuse at times and this really was too much. "I can't get this tie on straight!" he yelled.

My sister, Wijna, who also was still at home then at age eighteen, heard that, and she used to tease him mercilessly. Rien unawares yelled on, "Can't get this straight, my shoelaces are broken and knotted. I haven't got a pair of socks without a potato (hole) in it, oehhh this ruddy tie is strangling me."

Wijna saw her opportunity to have some fun. "Oh Riensy Beansy can't get his Bokketuigy on," (goatee tackle). That did it; Oh boy, all hell broke loose. He whinged and seethed and went for her. She ran upstairs through my bedroom, out through the door to the balcony. She got hold of the pear tree and swung on the branch before sliding down the tree trunk to the ground, with Rien in hot pursuit. The washing line full of sheets flapped wildly. They struggled and then ran again out into the road.

The Girl Who Saw Too Much

I guess Rien's tie and attire might have been a bit crumpled after that. I don't know if Wijna got a beating or not, but it was my bedtime again and Mum, when she got back, quite unperturbed sang my little bedtime song all the same.

Wijna later met her young man called Wim. He was very nice and they were obviously much in love. Still I thought they were a bit soppy together, kissing all the time, and holding hands. Wijna asked Mum and Dad to let them get married, but they thought her a bit too young yet. She was certainly quite grown up physically, and she begged them saying, "If we get more war trouble it will be harder for us and he is so nice and he has found an old little house a bit further up in our road. Oh please!" she wailed.

So they relented, and soon after her eighteenth birthday they were married. She looked beautiful in a lace dress, and Wim was so tall. I was to give Wijna her posy but he took it from me almost towering above me. Later they had two beautiful daughters and a lovely son, and I was an Aunty at eight years of age.

Helmi Wolff

The Silver Wedding Anniversary

On 28th April 1940, it was Mum and Dad's silver wedding anniversary.

It was exactly one week before the onset of WW II. Mum and my three sisters, Hanny, Nelly and Wijna, had been preparing a lovely musical short operetta of their own making, incorporating Mendelssohn's Wedding March to which Mum had put beautifully fitting words. They also made an archway of honour, dedicated to the happy couple, completely decorated with homemade crepe paper, roses and forget-me-nots. I was allowed to help make these, although I was only four years old. I loved the way each paper strip was wound around a fat knitting needle (no doubt borrowed from Mrs Vrederoord, the knitting queen of our road), and then stretched out along the needle and gathered at the other end into a rosette form. "They are so pretty and I like the red, white and blue colours," I said.

"Look, Mum, Mientje can do it!" said Hanny. "She made this one."

"Beautiful," said Mum. My cheeks glowed with pride and concentration for the job in hand.

"Tidy yourselves up now, you two," said Mum, addressing Frans and I. "Come here, Mien, I'll re-do your plaits with these ribbons. You two can deliver the invitations for the party, round the neighbours."

Proudly the homemade invitations were handed out which Frans had made and designed, each one with an elegant scrolling of a *25*, on bits of neat card.

"Here you are, Mrs Siemens, we have a party tonight, for Mother and Father's twenty-fifth wedding anniversary, please bring Mr Siemens as well."

"Hello, Mrs Backer, You know that you don't need an invitation for tonight as you are helping Mum and the girls to lay it all on for the party, but please bring Mr Backer of course." I was beginning to look a bit dubious at Frans as I wanted her especially to see the lovely invitations, then I looked at the old mantelpiece and saw one standing against the chimney breast already.

"Oh," is all I muttered.

Mrs Backer smiled, and popped a peppermint in my mouth, at which Frans yanked me out of the door to go on to the next house.

"One for you, Miss van Gareden, would your brother like to come too? You are very welcome."

"Mr van Biezen, this is an invitation to attend our party tonight, will your daughter, Lena, come along also?" Frans liked Lena, she was about his age and I had seen them walk together before, not surprising I thought, she had beautiful blonde curls, and starry blue eyes.

When the **'Ereboog'** (arch of honour) was put into place outside the front door, all the neighbours came to admire it and at the same time receive their invitation for the forthcoming event. I think everyone was welcome.

Our sitting room and front room were divided by large wooden sliding doors; these were then folded back making the room twice as big. Planks were carried in and 'saw horses' (they are wooden trestles and could be used as supports) were borrowed, to make two long trestle tables for everyone to sit at, that evening.

Sheets were a plenty and lots of plates and real glasses were set at each place, long planks on tree stumps were used for seats all covered with pillow slips and other nice bits of cloth.

Mum insisted that I had to sleep for a while. How could I calm down now to get sleepy? Freddy was brought into me for a special treat. I cuddled up with him in bed, as Mum really did not have time to sing me to sleep this time!

My beautiful navy blue taffeta dress was laid out ready for me to step into after a little 'cat nap'.

"Keep that pretty, white, lace colour clean now, Mien for tonight," Mum said, while she helped me buttoning up my new, black, lacquer shoes, which I adored, especially, because it made such a change from the high, lace up boots I usually wore.

Much later when a wonderful little operetta was performed, I realized that these pretty shoes were dancing shoes like my sisters wore for their performance. Han and Nelly also did *'quatre mains'* (four handed piano playing). It was so lovely that I decided to pay more attention to learning to play and perhaps Mum and I could perform something together.

As Frans had already learned to play the cornet quite well, at the Salvation Army, he performed a solo. Everyone clapped hands like they do at the Sally Army. Frans took a deep bow. Frans and Gerard wanted me to sit on the chair while they carried it aloft, but I got scared. I didn't like that; it was so wobbly. Dad's strong arms rescued me before I cried.

We all had beautiful, navy blue taffeta dresses with white collars, especially made for the occasion by each of my sisters themselves. Mum made hers and mine.

Both boys were also in navy blue with shirts and ties. Dad looked marvellous in his twenty-five-year-old navy pinstriped wedding suit, and his hair parted in the middle, which was the latest fashion. His moustache had been trimmed and sort of waxed in an upward flick.

The Girl Who Saw Too Much

The afternoon of that day was taken up with us going to the photographer in Apeldoorn. A much cherished photo in black and white, (sepia) was taken.

The photographer had a huge teddy bear with which he plied me to smile at the right time again and again. However, when it was time to go, he took Teddy away to shut it in a cupboard, which he closed with a bang, to my consternation.

People started to arrive, and as if by magic Mum poured a glass of lovely pink lemonade for each one. I saw Dad opening a bottle of something else. "A little fortification, Peter and Klaas?" Pa said.

"Oeh goo on then," replied one, while the other muttered,

"A little of what yer fancy ha?"

Mr Siemens handed his drink over to his wife; she took a tiny slug, nodded, and then handed it back to him. A lot of talk and laughter started from there on, and I noticed that the tiny glasses with funny drink stuff lasted all evening while they started to eat and drink.

Some little cakes appeared magically (to me) on a huge plate, carried by Hanny in her lovely new dress.

Nelly came in with another enormous long plate dressed out with a sort of salad, which I later found out, was called a 'Russian salad', although why that should be called Russian, when I had seen them prepare it in the kitchen became a puzzle to me, which Hanny later solved.

Fransien then sort of floated by in her rustling taffeta and lace dress, carrying a lot of individual small bowls with all sorts of sauces it seemed.

Lastly Wijna in her saved wedding dress made similar to ours with white lace collar, drifted in dreamily to set a big wedding cake made with real cream, like a gateau on the table.

All four were in position to serve everyone with the smashing food. I was told to sit still and wait till my turn came.

It was amazing that I did not feel hungry at all, with such an overly lot of delicacies in front of me, perhaps I was suffering my first attack of stage fright. At last it was my turn, and I was allowed to stand on a chair to sing the whole children's cantata with Mum, it was the one she sang for me almost every bedtime. We sang it with all the mannerisms of the play-park that the cantata was about. Everyone clapped when we finished.

Rien and Frans came in together carrying some wooden frames, which I had seen them working on in the shed last week.

Father noticed and winked at them. "Come on out from behind those, and when you have put them over there in a row," he commanded, while he gave them each a large full jug of a sort of great tasting lemonade. "You can both help me with pouring the drinks," said Pa.

By the time Mum and the girls were getting ready to do their performance in dance and music, I was in awe of all the people and food but not able to swallow any of the sweet offerings.

Mum was ready at the piano, and started to play the wedding march softly first, then louder when my sisters dressed as dancers came in.

Hanny, Nelly and Wijna each carried beautiful huge ornamental shapes in the form of a heart, an anchor and a cross, covered with lovely crepe paper roses and small flowers too.

Rien and Frans helped them to secure these against the wooden supports; 'Ah!' I thought, 'that is why they made those.'

The shapes were so big that my sisters were completely hidden behind them. When they reappeared, it seemed that the crepe paper roses, pink for the heart, blue for the anchor and white for the cross, representing faith, hope and charity, had enveloped them. How graceful this looked, with Mum playing the piano as they sang the words, which she had composed to blend in harmony. I was longing to grow up as beautiful as they were that day.

The Girl Who Saw Too Much

Dad had bought an old violin at an auction which none of us knew he could play. He proudly put it on his shoulder, with his chin on the casing, and struck the first notes with his bow.

I soon learnt the meaning of 'cat's meow'!

He got better after fiddling with the keys and screws at the bridge.

"So now, wife," he said, "we can try to play something together."

Oh boy, she tried something easy, but I believe they should have practised. It was fortunate that the neighbours were chatting amongst themselves.

So; Dad said, "It was just a bit of fun, I'll try later." I was so proud of him doing that so unexpectedly. He picked me up and said, "You thought your Dad had no music in him? I used to play as a boy at school and practise with the others."

When at last my bedtime came it was very late, probably 9.00 or 10.00 p.m. Mum put me to bed. She said, "You looked very pretty in your lovely dress and your hair curled with ribbons. I was very proud of you, singing with me."

We spread my new dress on the chair where I could admire it as I fell asleep. But at that point the door opened a crack, and Frans popped his head round the corner and said, "Mum, Dad is going to play his Stradie," as we jokingly called it. She hurried through my bedtime routine, tucked me in and left. If I hadn't been so tired I would have slipped out of bed, to sit at the top of the stairs listening,

But just before sleep overtook me I heard Dad play something like 'Hooray and up she rises early in the morning'. Then Mum accompanied him but it was in a different key. He hadn't tuned the Stradie to the piano I guess.

That night our little dog 'Freddy Fry', (so called after a famous war time correspondent), got up to some serious mischief. He had been neglected somewhat all day with the special goings on, plus he also had to put up with lots of strangers trooping in and out of the house.

He must have felt rather frustrated. While I was asleep he wandered around the house, came into my room and dragged my dress from my room. When I awoke in the morning, it was not there.

No one had the heart to tell me that Freddy had taken it to his basket and absolutely torn it to shreds.

Top row: Rien, Wijna, Nelly and Fransien
Bottom row: Hanny, Father, Mientje, Mum and Frans
Silver Wedding.

The Girl Who Saw Too Much

Mientje in her special little dress, on the motorbike.

Helmi Wolff

One week before the onset of WWII – on Mum and Dad's twenty-fifth wedding anniversary – Nelly and Wijna on Wim's motorbike, 28 April 1940.

The Girl Who Saw Too Much

A Royal Ovation, Early 1939

It was the custom in Apeldoorn, once a year on Queen Wilhelmina's birthday that all the school children would bring her a birthday ovation, singing Happy Birthday to her. I'd just started a sort of preschool, and I was so excited by the prospect of seeing the Queen. I was allowed with our little class to join with the others to march to the palace, in a very long procession. We were organized class by class in orderly rows to proceed along the *'Loo laan'*, which ended with that beautiful palace *'Het Loo'*.

It was a long way, and my teacher asked me if I wanted a piggy back, as she saw me limping a bit. "Oh no thank you, I can walk," I replied, much too proud to be carried indeed.

We sang as we went along, lots of school songs. But finally we reached the palace grounds, and the fantastically wrought iron golden gates opened for us to go through.

Guards with tall furry hats, watched us, standing dead still in front their funny little guardhouses, painted red and green. Suddenly they came out and shouted loud to each other after which they stamped their feet, and began to march to and fro, leaving a gap for us all to walk through in single file, right up to the white palace.

The teachers assembled us into long rows, the big ones at the back. We were right in the front. I hoped I would remember the words of the National Anthem, and the other special songs we had learned.

I'd seen Hanny and Frans among the older ones at the back, of course they must not talk to me, but I hoped they had seen me too.

While we waited, we watched the guards parading, and all of a sudden the teachers gave us little orange flags to wave, mine was a bit crinkled so I flapped it about to give it air.

Finally the upper balcony doors opened, and Queen Wilhelmina appeared, followed by Princess Juliana. We were ecstatic and we had to shout in unison like one voice: *"**Hoera for Oranje Boven, Hip hip hip hoera!**"*

At last the jubilant cry died down and the musical director had taken the small platform in front of us, he tapped his music stand and raised his baton.

We sang the National Anthem (Wilhelmus van Nassauwe), for which every one managed to stand quite still. After which we sang her birthday song, which goes a bit like this:

Someone today has a birthday hurrah
We all know who it is, it is her, hurrah
We are all so very glad for her hurrah, hurrah
That's why we're singing with joy,
May she live long, may she live strong
May she have joy hurrah, hurrah!

In Dutch;

Der is ter een jarig hoera hoera
dat kun je well zien dat is zy,
we vinden het allen zo prettig Ja ja,
en daaron zingen we bly,
ze leve lang [3 times] hoera [repeat]

The interesting bits with this birthday song are the mannerisms that were done with great enthusiasm by all of us. These go a bit like this: when the word *'zy'* (her) is sung, we all point to the birthday girl and the word *'hoera'* is shouted out loud for the Queen. It gives a great party spirit and feel of the performance.

The older children then sang two lovely Dutch songs about the country's beauty and Holland's endeavours, endurance and allegiance to the Royal family, all very well known and popular.

The one thing that amazed me was how everyone remembered all the words so well, but of course they had practised a lot before hand.

I never forgot that very special time. We were not to know that it would be the very last time for some very long years, that we could honour her, in this way that summer, because on May 5, 1940, war was declared by Germany, and all the Royal family had to escape to England and Canada for safety.

Still now I get a warm glow when I remember that I was allowed to stand in the front row dressed in my Sunday best white frock, with a lovely broad orange ribbon in my hair and one worn from the left shoulder to the hip, like a sash, where it was fastened, the same as all the children were given to wear by our school. And everyone in our best and shiny shoes, or newly painted wooden clogs, no holes in stockings or knee socks, the boys in their shirts and ties and respectable shorts.

It was just an outstanding and thrilling occasion; I thought we all looked like the smartest marchers and performers.

Helmi Wolff

Best Bib and Tucker

Spring 1940, just before the outset of WWII:
"Are you ready then, Mien?" called Dad. It was Sunday and I was struggling with my boots. Why were they always giving me jib when I was in a hurry? Looking at my attempts to tie the laces with a neat bow, Dad said, "Come here, and let me do that for you."

Oh thank goodness I had got into a flap, and my cheeks were glowing with concentration.

It was quite a rigmarole getting ready for the posh church where everyone wore their Sunday best as if they had that on all the time.

I was only four years of age, going to the grandest church in Apeldoorn; it was even called **'Grote Kerk'** (Big Church).

The most significant time being the occasion when Queen Wilhelmina together with Princess Juliana and ladies in waiting visited, to take part in the service.

Walking out with Dad dressed in his navy pinstripe suit under his smart warm coat, and his fashionable walking cane, with beige felt spats over his shiny shoes; I thought he was the best-dressed, most handsome father I knew.

I tried to keep in step with him. Quite impossible of course, so I drifted away a little, to skip through the grass and leaves at the sides happily.

Dressed in my best coat and hat, which Mum had made from a grey blanket lined with the lovely blue and orange flower silk that was once her summer dress. It also had a double row of small shell-like metal buttons on one side and sort of loops, called **'trenches'**, on the other side, right up to the little collar, high up on the neck, which was very neat, but if my hands were freezing cold, it was near impossible to fasten all ten of them.

Dad had a go once and said, "This is quite a rigmarole, Mien." I did love the navy and white little flowers she had embroidered on the sides of the hat even if the rough material was a bit prickly.

Once just as we were about to leave, Dad suddenly spotted the red nail varnish on my nails. Earlier Hanny, being in a generous mood, had allowed me to look at her lipsticks and nail varnishes. There were bright pink and transparent ones, and of course I chose the RED. "Well, we have to scrub that off now, with Vim or Ajax and a nailbrush," said Dad. My fingers were raw with the scrubbing, before we embarked on our one kilometre walk to church.

Father's boudoir and grooming was interesting too. He had a magnificent moustache with points like Jimmy Edwards and it must have been a tricky business keeping it neat with the slash razor he used, which he sharpened on a leather strip coated with pumice stone powder. Of course all this was done in private, but one day I slipped into the kitchen, which doubled as bathroom, for washing. Both my parents had dentures at an early age, but I'd never seen either of them without them.

Imagine my astonishment when Dad took his teeth out and proceeded to brush them under the tap. I thought that was a terrific party trick. Once, when we had jolly visitors I asked, "Dad, do that trick with your teeth again." But Dad said, "Hush now, we don't talk about that!"

Dad liked to see me happy but this time he said, "You can't wear your shoe leather out quick enough, can you?" That's when I realized that it was not just fun for him, mending the soles of my boots.

Then I remembered him hammering away on all of our shoes, with a heavy iron last to sit them on, while he sorted out the tiny nails needed for the job. Pulling off the old shoe sole to cut into smaller heal and toe buffer bits. He then cut the new soles from a large piece of leather, with a very small knife that he had sharpened on the turn stone the day before, with me pouring a trickle of water over it, while I also turned the handle round and round. Ah but I knew I'd get a nice peppermint or boiled sweet afterwards.

Once, one of the tiny nails was sticking up through the inner sole of my special boot. It was painful and I had to wear them for the day at school, making my stunted running even slower as I limped my way through rounders.

Then the thought of Frans shining all our shoes on the Saturday evening before we all got bathed, ready for Sunday and the following school days.

I stopped skipping and held on to Dad's hand; after all it was quite a daunting experience when we neared the huge church with all the people streaming in, and every one looking so grand.

The church had several entrances, but we always entered through the main one, with the beautiful archway adorned with angels above it. However this time Royal guards, named *'Huzaren'*, were standing at the entrance and two policemen ushered people through the other doors. It left me a bit puzzled when Dad told me that I had to be extra good and quiet, as we were very honoured to be able to see the Queen in our midst.

'Grote Kerk' (Big Church).

Entering now at the opposite side from where we usually did, I looked in amazement at everything being in a different place it seemed.

As soon as we sat down, a hush fell over the congregation, and Queen Wilhelmina with her entourage took their seats in the 'Royal box'; a box being a terrible understatement, as this beautiful polished wooden area was so intricately carved with every kind of Royal head and flower.

Every one stood as we sang the Dutch royal anthem, with our left hand on our heart, this was all new to me in church.

Queen Wilhelmina stood up smiling and waved to acknowledge everyone, after which we sat down and the proper service began with the great pipe organ playing beautiful music. I was so impressed that I forgot the little sweets Mum had put into a tiny silver box for me.

"Dad," I whispered, "that must have been a lot of work moving that huge pipe organ from one wall to another."

Dad looked at me and said, "Sshh." He gave me a sweetie out of his pocket, but I was not satisfied with that, so off I went again with, "But Dad, look at the pulpit. He is preaching from the other side now!" "Ssshhh." I was given a piece of paper, and a small pencil to do some drawing, which I loved to do, but it still puzzled me a lot.

The next Sunday it was Mum's turn to take me to her much smaller church, She had her old blue hat re-decorated with a cream scrunched up ribbon done like little pleats around the front, which gave it a new appearance.

Her church was a small hall called ***Patrimonium.*** It was a much livelier smaller group of people, who confided in each other all their needs and wishes in their long prayers. They also addressed each other as Brother and Sister 'so and so', which I found strange, as I knew that Mum's sisters were not there, and lived a long way away now.

Mum played the harmonium at her church, so we always had to arrive a little earlier than the rest.

"Sister Wolff, the organ is ready," said Brother Peters, as this mobile harmonium had to be brought in each time. Mum sat down, and I stood beside her, as it was my job to turn the music pages of the hymn book, a job I took very seriously, as I was quite proud to be able to read the music a little, even at that young age. Luckily Mother always nodded at the right spot for me to turn the page, **'*now!*'**

Prayer time was very serious, and people just stood up when they were ready. I was given some paper and a small pencil again, but I found quietly listening to the people very interesting and amazing, if I could of course, with folded hands and eyes closed.

Mr Van Straten, an elderly bald headed gentleman, regularly begged for all his troubles to vanish, and as he bared his soul, listing the wishes for himself, his daughters, aunts, uncles, neighbours and his wife, I got more and more interested, and I wondered if Vickie and I could use it in our great play saga about our pretend family later.

Another lady of great interest was Juffrouw Stemedink. She always wore a brown hat, coat and shoes, and looked quite prim and proper. When she opened up, she was like a flower needing rain.

She had an elderly father, to look after, who was very demanding of her attention all the time. She felt it her duty to clean, shave and feed him and put him to bed. She seemed such a lonely person without any love in her life. At the meetings she felt a bond with the other kind members of the congregation, and when she left, she would always give me a wet kiss on both cheeks, which I didn't dare wipe off, as she told Mum what a good girl I had been.

Glowing with self-esteem and with little notes adapted for our play, we were off to meet Dad.

The small trim of my hat was sagging over my left eye, and that is why I had not spotted Hanny first, with her little boyfriend standing across the road looking into a shop window. I was surprised that mother quickened her step; I looked to see, and twigged the whole thing. Mum pretended she had not seen her, but I believe that she was asked later about the service in the Salvation Army she should have attended.

Dad was waiting for us. It was our custom to visit family in that area after church for coffee. This time it was the turn for Aunt Anny and her two beautiful daughters. My aunt baked gorgeous cakes and I was always hungry. Mum usually played requests on their piano, such as **'Ave Maria',** or **'Jerusalem'** or even **'Roselein auf der heide'.** It was like a cosy party. I observed their hair styles and decided that when I grew up I also would have my hair in a long winding sausage roll from the neck all round the sides and up to the top of the head, culminating into a cute little kiss curl springing from the high bit in the front.

Other times we visited Aunt Ko. That was nice too, but she was really strict and old-fashioned in her clothes and house decor. She lived above a furniture shop and had been a schoolmistress for many years, but she usually had lovely biscuits. My favourite were those crispy sponge fingers sprinkled with sugar and cinnamon and I absolutely adored her coffee as she spooned a good dollop of cream into the steaming cups.

Sometimes it was our turn to have people over after church. I did not mind most of them, but there was a lady with her husband who obviously were not used to children. They never even looked at me and I was told then, to go and read, or have some time for play in my room, while I knew that all the goodies were served downstairs. Mum usually brought me something nice up to share with Freddy and my dolls – ah well!

Sundays were busy for me anyhow, because after lunch it was Sunday school time. We walked all the way there to a big re-vamped shed, a few blocks from our homes. Arm in arm with my friend, Vicky, both still in our best clothes, we felt like 'Kingpins', saying hello and howdy to anyone on the way. We were looking forward to the stories the two ladies in charge always read to us from a big colourfully illustrated children's bible, from a faraway land where the sun always shone and everyone wore sandals. Afterwards we were all given a small picture the size of a postage stamp, to accompany the story we had just been told.

Every child had been given a small album with the shortened stories, in which there were places to stick your stamp. If you missed Sunday school, you also missed the stamp for your collection. At Christmas time the child with the most stamps was rewarded with a lovely bookmarker.

The Girl Who Saw Too Much

Mum and Hanny, me at the back, in front of our house.

Helmi Wolff

The Neighbours and Us, Knikkers!

About ten houses up in the Bartels weg on the opposite side of the road lived the Kindemans, a family consisting of mother, father, brother and two daughters, Atie, eight years and Bieky, nine years.

Atie was small for her age, rather shy and unassuming. She was dominated by her older sister, Bieky, who was big for her age, and (I found) had a sly cunning way with her.

To my thinking, she was such an unpleasant girl; she would be the one who had to win every game and brag about it. She also hit her sister a lot and then told fibs about it to her tiny mother, causing Atie even more problems. She'd worm her way in on any secret or plan and then twist it to suit herself.

One day I'd been given a whole new bag of **knikkers** – these were small clay balls about three millimetres in diameter, everyone a nice different colour, plus one or two ***stuiters*** (glass marbles).

The game of **knikkeren** was a very serious occupation, as the winner would get the entire pot of knikkers, however many there were in it at that time, a game of luck and skill.

We were playing in front of my house and I had made a small dip in the sand with my heel for, The Pot.

All of us smoothed the surrounding earth for a trouble free run. We won in turns more or less, until Bieky came out and said that our dip was stupid; she made another much deeper one and got us all to play for higher stakes and when almost all our knikkers were in the pot. "Now it is my turn, but first," she said, "the earth is uneven." So she smoothed it extra fine for herself. She won the whole pot with practically all my new knikkers in it.

We all objected and when she pushed over her sister, I got furious and picked up some of my knikkers, and in throwing them at her, sort of accidentally hit her on the head just above her eyebrow. Oh now I'd done it, for a moment I stood nailed to the ground and so did she, amazed at the accuracy I think. I thought she was going for me, but she must have been so put out, that she turned on her heels and ran down the street to her house, actually crying all the way.

I was so flabbergasted at my aim, when fear gripped me, and I knew to make myself scarce.

She was twice my size and the Kindemans were a formidable mop of fearful people; quick hide somewhere, I ran home and into my room upstairs pretending to do my school homework. About five minutes elapsed, when suddenly a great banging on the front door gave me such a start. Scared stiff I peeked out of the window, and there they all were, the entire Kindemans family, even the Gran, with Bieky at the front sporting a swelling on her forehead the size of a small bird's egg.

I was shaking in my shoes, when I heard Mother opening the front door. "Look what Mientje has done to our daughter," boomed Mr Kindeman; they were all trying to get through the narrow door opening on the stoop, all shouting at once about the Wolff's wayward daughter despite Mother's attempt in saying that she would be punished.

They were not to be fobbed off, yelling and pushing, shouting, "Where is Mr Wolff? We seen he come home, he 'as to beat the livin' daylights out o' 'er."

Helmi Wolff

Mum, me, Wijna, Hanny, and Dad, with little Mia in front.

The Girl Who Saw Too Much

I had never had as much as a tick on my bum from either Mum or Dad, and poor old Dad had to think quickly. Mum closed the front door and called me down; she stuffed some soft washing in the back of my pants, and told Dad, that he was to give me a beating with the *'matten-klopper'*, (a willow carpet beater).

Out the back door Dad said to me, "Howl when I beat you." Bewildered I saw that they had all come to see 'Fair Play', so to speak. Dad got me over his knee with a great show of bravado and started to rain the twine beater down onto my pants.

No one need have told me to howl, the whole thing was so degrading; I jumped every time contact was made with my bony little bum. It shocked me to the core and I cried for an hour afterwards, although no marks were left on me at all. I realized afterwards that a great show of pretence was made and the blows softly delivered.

I was comforted, but also warned sternly by both, never, ever to do that again.

Other Neighbours

On another occasion, Atie and Bieky, were allowed to wheel their beautiful dolls pram and proper china dolls in them out onto the road to show them off, while Grandma watched from their doorway.

Never in my life had I seen such beautiful dolls dressed in the loveliest satin and lace. The pram had an up and down hood and the body of the pram was worked with lovely ornate swirls and patterns. It also had real little tyres on the sturdy quite large wheels. I was enthralled with the pretty clothes, properly lined with fine cotton lawn and more lace.

All that at a time when coupons would not even buy the merest bit of cloth to make proper clothes for people or a new skirt or bodice, stockings or elastic, not that I realized that. The dolls were clothed in such luxury: I think that I swooned.

But what I could not understand is that while that family seemed to live in real poverty compared to mine, how was it that they had such a treasure? Later I was told that they were only allowed outside with it for half an hour, and that was an even bigger mystery to me when, if we should have had such a lovely thing, I would have been allowed to play with it carefully whenever I could. Atie also told me that these dolls and perambulator had belonged to their Gran and her sister.

More neighbours.

Next door to the Kindemans lived Juffrouw (Mrs) Smeenk with her little daughter, Leenie; she was a year older than me. I never saw Mr Smeenk, but she was a fine dressmaker and Leenie always wore the most marvellous handmade fashionable clothes.

I remember a red velvet dress with swansdown all around the hem, sleeves and neckline, which I admired so much.

Another wonderful little dress Leenie wore was a tiny black and white check dress with little shell buttons all down the front. When she grew out of that, Mrs Smeenk asked Mum if she wanted it for me. "Ohhh yes please," I was over the moon. It was rather roomy on my thin little frame, but Mum did a bit of magic with the velvet belt and a pretty clasp at the front.

I loved wearing it, and as Leenie did not attend our school anyway, it was like brand new, and it made a welcome change for me, not to have to wear my older sister's hand-me-downs, which were made a bit shorter and smaller by Mum and Hanny sometimes. Kids notice these things and can be horribly cruel about it.

The Girl Who Saw Too Much

Even more neighbours

At the top of our road lived the Lavenswaai family; there were thirteen children all much older than me. My eldest brother, Rien, had been friends with Piet Lavenswaai, which Mum was not too keen on, as they fraternised with quite a rough crowd and Piet easily led Rien into trouble frequently with his impressionable and sweet nature.

Some of them had been up to nicking here and there, and when trouble flared, they blamed it on Rien.

Well my brother saw red, tempers flared and an almighty fight broke out between them. Rien came off worse and had quite a nasty head wound, which stayed a large scar. Rien decided to leave home, and literally join the circus as a labourer.

Apparently, at one time he was fixing the centre pole in the top nook, (no safety net). He fell to the ground and dislocated or badly injured his neck. He was critically ill in hospital for a long time, but recovered well although it still troubled him often during his lifetime.

One episode this family was involved in concerned me directly. Hanny had made a lovely rag doll for me, with bright yellow gown and slippers made of her own blouse, I loved it and was displaying it to all who were interested, wanting them to admire my doll.

One such a person was Gerda Lavenswaai (Piet's sister). She pretended to be interested asking if she could hold it, to which I readily agreed, but then all of a sudden she ran away with it. Devastated and in tears I told Mum. "Right," she said, "we'll see about that." Taking me by the hand we marched off to the top of the road and into the gate of their house. Mrs Lavenswaai all ready stood cockily at the front door,

"Ya?" she said more than asked. Mum told her what had happened and I was sent back to outside the gate, while a rather heated conversation ensued. All I could hear were bad words from Mrs L., but when I heard the word 'beer put', which is cesspit, I feared the worst, and yes they had drowned my lovely doll in it.

Mother was appalled, and told them to fish it out, and clean it up. Piet was called and the next thing that happened made such a dreadful smell that I had to move, so I never saw the filthy doll. Mum told Mrs L. to wash it thoroughly and return it to us, which she did, but I never took to it again.

Towing this exhibition vehicle with contents (Mother's snow-white baby napkins; little vests etc.) for the 'Klork Zeep' company, very like Sunlight or Green Soap Powder. Gramophone music was playing. People came to see and hear Dad's advertising.

The Girl Who Saw Too Much

Electricity in Our House

Just before the war this great new invention in our house called ELECTRICITY was a masterstroke of which Dad was mighty proud. He had to lay on a little light for my Gran just before the war, as she was ill and needed to see her way at night when she had to get up so often.

Mum who thought that Dad could fix anything, asked him to show what he could do for Gran.

It was only a little bicycle light but as Gran said, "We have to count the pennies, and that way I can see, and it won't hurt the purse too much." I was told that Gran was not plentiful with her praise, and this was probably as far as she would go, I can believe that.

Dad glowed brighter than the little bulb; such was praise indeed from the matriarch of the clan, but more praise in the form of advertising was to come. All round the neighbourhood he was now known as, 'The first; the only, fully fledged electrician'. Everyone wanted him to lay on this electric magic in their homes.

When Dad had a new job, and after he came home from his rather tiresome work of helping to build a great grotto and tunnel in the local park, he found a new pastime with this electricity, which he did for a nice cup of coffee and a chat, but most important to him was that little Freddy, our dog, would be allowed to lick a little of the sweetest coffee from the saucer at the end.

That dog knew! As soon as he saw Dad he was impatient to come along on his newfound occupation.

Ours was the show house, having an ELECTRIC light in every room, even the indoor toilet now had a little glow worm as we called it. Mum said you don't really need a light to pull up your knickers, but it is nice to know that you can see the doorknob.

I sure agreed to that, as I had an abhorrence of the dark ever since Vickey's Mum told me that there was a Boo-man in the dark and that he came in through the letterbox. It scared me a lot; even though I was told not to be silly and that there was no such a thing.

I used to go to the loo as fast as I could, to get back into the proper light, but always trying to look calm and relaxed as if I had no fear at all.

Dad used every bit of left over electric wire, from jobs he had done, consequently a room at a time was installed with the wonderful, new light. Obviously, he installed the main ones first.

The bits of wire were not always long enough so the marvellous insulation tape was used to fuse two bits of wire together.

Frans was told not to borrow a bit of the windings for his kites or his photographic enterprises, or anything else.

To make sure of the safety of the apparatus Dad laid the wires high onto the wide dado rail shelves and secured them with little tags to keep it all in place. This was also the place where Mother kept her fine china like Gran's teapot and her best vases etc.

From the junctions of the wires he would drop a third one down where it could be reached to put on a socket for a plug. Mum now was the proud owner of one of the first cylinder sausage vacuum cleaners. It was truly marvellous, no one else had one but Dad bought this one in an auction for her.

"Well," he said. "Wife, now you don't have to go round on your sore knees to brush up the dust." What a great help that was. The first time she used it she thought that she still had to use the damp sprinkled tea leaves. Well you can guess what happened, the insulation of the new marvel was not so sturdy, thus a fuse blew as soon as she used it. *Oh calamity*, but it was fixed and the next time was perfect, except that it would not pick up anything heavier than the smallest button, which was just as well for buttons were another expensive commodity. Of course bits of paper and large fluff blocked the long rubber tube, which was often my job to unblock. "Come on, Mien, your little fingers are small enough to get in there."

The biggest commotion was caused by Hanny, who looking for the tiny little stone which had come out of her ring, was told that the marvellous vacuum cleaner had been used that day, and maybe it had been sucked up by it. Wailing she got the offending machine, took it outside and we all tried to sift and find the tiny red stone with her, but to no avail. Returning to her room we heard a loud shout of triumph, as she had found it where she had hidden it behind her make-up. "Oh boy," said Frans, "that could only happen to girls!"

Mum and I were trying to come to grips with my organ lessons. Trying to keep the right rhythm was not that easy, it meant that I had to go slow to be able to sustain the right pace, "One, two, three, four."

"Yes I know, but I want to give it a bit more oomph."

"Well perhaps you would be better off with a steam organ?" Frans interrupted.

"What's that?" I asked.

"Well you know, you see the one that comes through our road sometimes."

"Oh that is a 'Draai organ', you turn the handle like the man does, sometimes he has a monkey on a chain I don't know why, or what he is to do with it."

"Well he collects the money."

I had only seen this once; I expect ours was not a wealthy enough neighbourhood for him to bother with too often.

Just as we got going again with the organ music, Dad came home. "Guess what," he said. "I have something for us all to use."

"Is it electric?" Mum asked.

"Well of course, we are in the new age now, Wife, and we aren't going back you know," as he winked at me he disappeared into the kitchen, we were so curious.

"So," he said very importantly, "you see this amazing apparatus, Wife?" Oh yes we did, it was a toaster. "This is a toaster," he announced. "See, you plug it into the new socket I have just fixed and voila, at that." A sort of sizzling sound was heard and a short put-put, of smoke went up. "Oeh," we blurted.

"Ah, ah, just a minute," Dad mumbled while he walked to his shed.

"That could be lovely," Mum, said – when he has fixed it!

When Dad was called for his supper he had mended the fuse. Tucking the toaster under his arm he said, "Wait till I show you, you will never have to stand over a hot stove to toast bread again."

Now it truly was the most used gadget ever, even if we did not know then that the asbestos with mica covering all over the element in the centre to heat the bread on both sides at once of the small opening doors, was to become a health hazard.

The celebrated toaster tied with the electric iron for first place, which was a much later edition. I remember Mother saying when we had visitors, to me, "I hope the ELECTRIC iron and the ELECTRIC toaster are not left on?"

The Girl Who Saw Too Much

The Occupation

One of the first sights of the occupation we were treated to was goose-stepping. Like a machine they marched and stamped through our village, at least a hundred German soldiers, in black uniforms with red trimmings and gleaming stiff black leather knee-high boots. These boots were equipped with metal heel and toe pieces to make a rattling, clinking noise as the soldiers goose-stepped along.

Of course, when we first saw this type of marching we had no idea what it was called, but it shocked fear into everyone who witnessed it. Not one smile or smirk was to be seen on the villagers' faces. It seemed like an evil show of power, constructed to strike awe into every heart and head. It was as if they were saying, "We are in charge here now and we will not stand any nonsense or resistance. We will rule you with an iron fist and plunder you until you have nothing and no one left."

The message was loud and clear, more so than any words could convey, and that so soon after they had slain most of the brave fighters on **'Grebbe Berg',** where Holland was totally unprepared to outdo such a mighty force as invaded our country. Our men were completely outmanoeuvred and killed. Those who survived that bloody battle were transported to the German prisoner-of-war camps. Some were used for experimentation, others put to hard labour, most of them never to return home.

Mum, Hanny, Frans and I watched the macabre goose-stepping machine through our front window. I could feel the drone of the metal caps hitting the road, pass though my whole body. Mum had her arms around us, tears trickling down her face. We all felt totally lame to say or do anything. I was only four and a half and it stunned me to see such a hateful display. It was never to be forgotten.

We knew their intention was, to say the least, to instil fear into everyone and to intimidate us. Sometimes, in my early nightmares, flashes of that sight would intersperse with hooting trains full of innocent Jewish people, guns, fighting planes, and bombs falling all in a childish perception of horror. But I know now that the Dutch are a wiry bunch, not so easily beaten or discouraged.

Dad and Rien, had long been working on a beautiful park called **'Berg en Bos'** (Hills and Woods). The hills were artificially created with the earth that came out of the lake they made. It was a hard time for the men in our village but they were glad to get the work as the slump had hit everyone badly. They also made a huge tunnel with a waterfall above it. Enormous rocks and stones were needed for this, which all had to be lifted by hand as machinery for that purpose had not yet been invented, at least not in our village. Our men were just cheap labour at the time.

One evening Dad and Rien had only just washed themselves after coming home at about 7.00 p.m. when the cry went up from outside at the top of the road. Mother was just going to serve the supper for that evening and shouted, "Quick hide, the Gestapo is coming." But it was too late and two grizzly looking German soldiers burst into our house through the big French window doors which had been left open for fresh air. They could see Dad and Rien from the open doors; they were trapped.

The soldiers looked at us all and bullied, "You and you," pointing at Dad and Rien. "Come with us." They pointed their guns at us all and looked menacing. Resisting the order was pointless. Mum ran to Dad and held him as if that could keep him with us. Poor Rien, white as a sheet, just kissed Hanny and I, and hugged Frans, Mum and Dad. There was no escaping their fate.

The Girl Who Saw Too Much

Daddy held me for a while and said, "Now, Mien, you are a big girl already and you can draw lovely pictures for me, so write to me that way huh?" I promised but where was he going? He kissed me goodbye, struggling to hold back his own tears. We were perplexed, in tears and sobbing too. No one knew where they were going or how. Would we ever see them again? Mum fell on her knees and prayed fervently for their safe return to us.

We ran outside with them and saw at least half a dozen other men torn away from their families. Their faces said it all, but I think the worst parting that I saw was just across the road where a young couple with a baby had only just come to live. The lovely young woman would not let her husband go and it was barbaric the way the soldiers tore her man away from her. I was shocked to the core and Mum rushed us all inside quickly.

Mum promised Dad that she would find him somehow, and find him she did, a lot later, but that is another story.

We had no knowledge of their whereabouts after they were all marched out of our road, but neighbours had seen them being loaded into cattle trucks of the long, waiting train which then went east. We had to live with the uncertainty of their safety and there were many times I asked Mum if they were all right. It made her so sad, and every night when she tucked me into bed we would pray for their safe return.

And then... after two and a half months, a letter arrived. Mother's hands were trembling as she opened the envelope. It was from Dad and Rien. Oh wonderful. After all that worrying and grieving, not knowing or hearing where and how they were, we were overjoyed. My heart skipped a beat when I spotted Dad's flourishing handwriting. Rien had written too. Hanny and Frans were standing behind Mum trying to read over her shoulder. "Oh thank God," she shouted, "they're alright."

"Where are they, Mum?" I shouted.

"Well it's a place called Düsseldorf, not so very far over the border, and they have been placed in a sort of workhouse where they sleep, but Dad has a lorry."

"A lorry?" marvelled Frans.

"He has to help pick up the rubble after the bombings and get the people out alive or dead, and Rien has been placed in a sawmill factory to make wooden sheds and shelters for the barracks."

We did not know then that the sheds and shelters were mostly to make the death camps for the Jewish people, nor did we know that he had sawn off two fingers of his right hand.

He had run to the militarily hospital where they told him to run back and find his fingers in the sawdust, which he did, and they stitched them back on in the hospital. His fingers had healed by the time we received the letter, although somewhat crooked, but later he told us that he had found an accordion and was able to play it, crooked fingers or not.

But we were reading the marvellous letter, and as we put it down Mum began to jump and march round and round the table and we all joined in. Frans scooped me up and I was handed from him to Han and Mum, shouting and singing, ***"Daddy and Rien are safe and good."*** I struggled to be free and leapt ahead, running madly, happily in front. Mother even started banging the table with the forks, knives and spoons, in rhythm to 'Lang zal die leven cookies zal die geven'. (Long may he live and give us many cookies.) It was fantastic. The neighbours who heard all the commotion, rushed in to see us all dancing and singing with joy, and a letter flapping wildly in Mum's hands.

When we showed it to them, and said that Dad and Rien were well, they all joined in and soon the room was full. I don't know where Mum got the weak tea, perhaps it was our weekly ration, but everyone sat down where they could and a lot of hugging went on and 'Well I never', and 'Marvellous'. "Thank God," my mother said.

After that, more letters arrived but they were still few and far between because they were not allowed to send more. Also, every letter was scrutinized there and no objects were allowed to be included like a photo or lock of hair, but we learned that they had been moved to different sleeping quarters with running water and a stove to cook on. They were to be moved on to different accommodation many times so our letters with my drawings were often sent from pillar to post and often took a long time to reach them, causing them a lot of anguish too.

Helmi Wolff

Lieve Papa en Rien   **April 1941, I was 5 years of age.**

Mamma took me to a lovely little school, it is called kinder garden. There was Mrs Verhoes en Mrs Grevestuk. They have some lovely toys for me and other children to play with. There was a little boy called Tienus and he let me help with wooden bricks He let me put a little arch on top of it to make a doorway, and then also a chimney, it looked nice, but Anneke knocked it down and he cried.

    Later we all joined hands and did a dancing game called stamp your feet like ring a roses, we had to choose a friend to dance with, Anneke choose me but I liked Lena best.

    We got a lovely hot drink and a yellow biscuit, I missed Mamma a bit but she came early, to watch us play, she helped me with a drawing to show you.

    Do you have a lorry there, maybe you can ride it back to us please we miss you so much.

    Hugs from us all

    Mamma wrote this for me, course I can't do that yet, but I told her Bye,

Mientje xxxxx

The Girl Who Saw Too Much

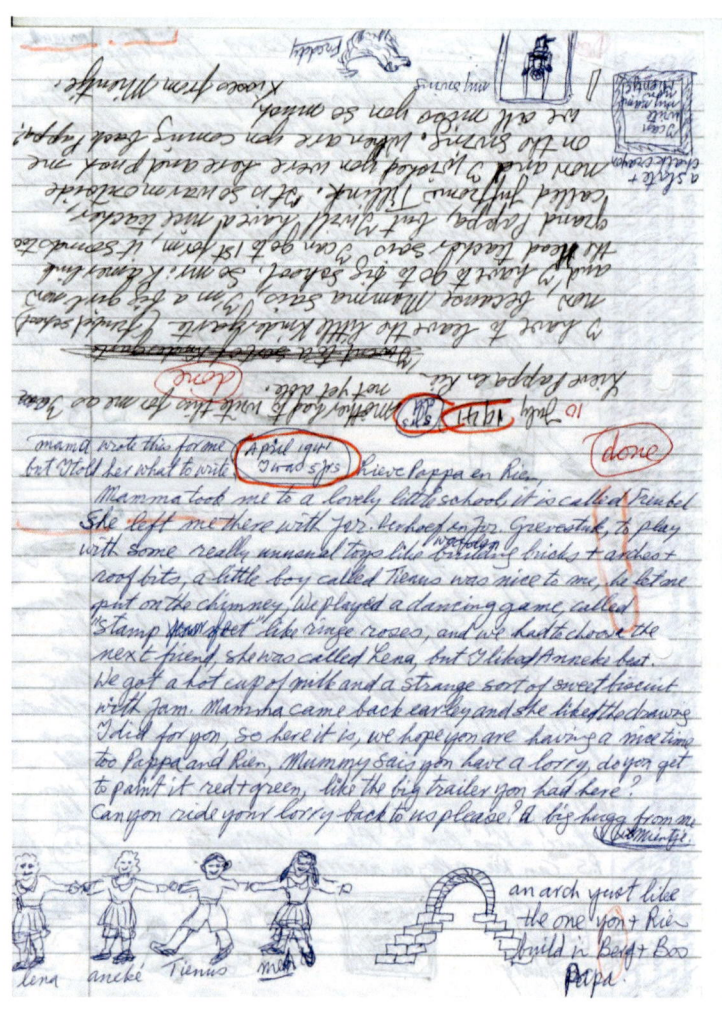

Helmi Wolff

Lieve Pappa en Rien   Dec. 1941

Today those soldiers came marching through our road again. They did funny high steps with straight legs. Their boots made a loud clatter, like iron, I wished they wouldn't do that, it is frightening as if they are so angry with us, I don't think they like us, and I don't like them either. Frans told me that it is called goos stepping.

How are you Daddy and Rien, have you got nice food to eat? We were given some sugar beet by Mrs Stammers, Mum cooked them a lot on the Range and now we have sweet syrup to put on our pap. Hope you come home soon Papa.

Love, Mientje.

The Girl Who Saw Too Much

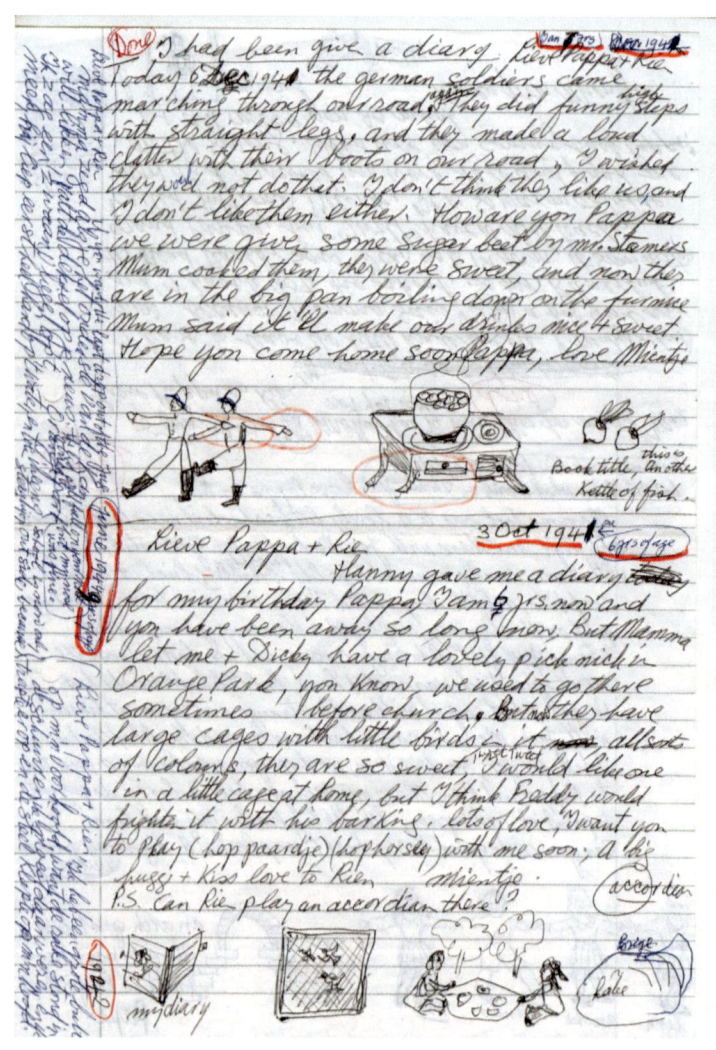

Helmi Wolff

The Girl Who Saw Too Much

New Year's Day

A great custom on New Year's Day was for the children to go around the neighbourhood saying, "Gelukig Nieuw Yoar, bint de poffertjes all kloar," meaning Happy New Year, are the oily buns ready? in full Apeldoorn dialect. Oily buns were lovely, being invariably filled with either a slice of apple or dried fruit, then dipped into batter and deep fried. They were something like small pancakes filled with mincemeat or other fresh fruit and fried like dumplings called *'olie bollen'*.

Frans thought he'd take me along, to perhaps get twice as much with a cute little five-year-old in tow. "Now," he said. "When I knock on the doors you have to go to the front and smile while I wish them a Happy New Year." But first we had to get to the chosen houses.

Half walking, half running, we got to the first one. Mrs Ravelaar said, "I ain't got no oil to make 'um, and tell yer Mum she's put yer hat on back to front." Whereupon I took off my hat to examine it, but found nothing wrong with it. She burst out laughing to see my cross face.

I looked at her huge gaping mouth, showing a few ugly remaining yellow teeth, and somehow I lost my appetite for anything she might have baked. Frans looked cross too as he helped me to button up the chinstrap on my homemade hat. No luck there then, I thought.

"We'll go and see Aunty Marie," Frans decided.

"Oh," I mumbled. I hardly knew her. Her husband Uncle Jaap had a bicycle shop. They only lived a few roads away.

Helmi Wolff

The Girl Who Saw Too Much

We had to cross two main roads, and Frans took me by the hand, almost dragging me along. My little legs were aching, and my left foot was clumping a bit. He stopped to consider whether he could drag me any further and, with a sudden burst of inspiration, said, "Come on, Mien, and climb on to my shoulders."

"Oh great," I gushed. Just then we saw a little man approaching at the opposite end of the road.

"Right," said Frans, "that is Sellemessy." That name sent fear into me, especially when he explained that he got that name because of the little knife he always carried, and if he didn't like someone he would threaten them with it.

Sellemessy was a seriously disturbed man and seeing him scared me a lot. You should just leave him alone I thought, and then he'd go his own way.

Frans told me not to look his way, and then, he blurted out, "Sellemessy." I suppose it was too much for him to miss out on the excitement.

Breaking out into a gallop, with me on his shoulders, he ran as fast as he could, but Sellemessy was gaining.

I looked back and saw him run at a funny sideways gallop, shouting all sorts of abuse and hurling a stone. Luckily he missed but by now I think even Frans was scared.

Suddenly Frans shot into a side ally where he knew a place, just round the corner, with a sort of alcove to hide in, where Sellemessy could not see us. We saw him steaming by, shouting and cursing.

His face had turned a dark shade of red. All this time Frans held his hand over my mouth and I was almost choking. He took his hand away at last, and I was glad to breathe normally again.

We stayed there for at least ten minutes, being as quiet as mice, only breathing, with no talking.

Eventually we ventured out to see if the coast was clear. There was no one to be seen, so we set off again in the direction of Aunty

Marie's house. It was a relief to arrive there, and, seeing us coming from her window, she opened the door before we had time to knock.

"Oh how lovely, come in children," she said warmly. "Are you hungry?" she asked.

"Oh yes, Tante Marie. We came to wish you both a Happy New Year," Frans said. He went on to tell her of our daring exploits, on our way over to see them. Uncle Jaap picked me up and sat me on his lap.

"How old are you now, Mientje?" he asked.

"Five," I said.

"Ohhh," came the reply.

We all watched Aunt Marie sprinkling powdered icing sugar over the scrumptious oily buns, which made them look as if they had been dusted with snow. They looked even more inviting than anything I had seen in the baker's window.

Tucking in, she asked, "How's your Mum and Dad? And your sisters and brothers?" We said they were all fine and getting a little food on the coupons and that Hanny was staying with some friends for a few days. We also told her that Nelly was staying with Fransien in a big town and Mum was making a new dress for me.

After a bit more nice banter, our sweet aunt offered us a second helping, which was gratefully accepted by both of us. She then sat herself down at the piano and played some lovely seasonable songs for us, while we tried to sing along.

After a while, fortified and rested, we made to go back home again, but she said, "Uncle Jaap is going to take you on the back of his bike as I don't want you to repeat that awful escapade again."

Uncle Jaap had a huge bicycle, with a large carrier front and back. After some sort of cushion mat was put on both, I was lifted onto the front and Frans climbed onto the back. Uncle Jaap peddled so fast I thought we were flying. We reached home in no time at all. I'd hoped our Uncle Jaap would come in but he said he had quite a lot of work in his cycle shed, so he didn't.

I remember Hanny taking her bicycle to his shop for repairs. I think her chain kept coming off when she had a puncture. Of course if Dad had still been home, he would have done that for her. Dad did a lot of repairs in our own shed.

I remembered that Hanny had peddled me to Uncle Jaap's before, so I'd seen his workshop at the back of their house.

On *that* short journey we had encountered another Apeldoorn character.

This man was known as **'Pon Pearde Lappen', (pound of horse meat),** a cruel name for a very large mentally handicapped man, who had also got scalded with boiling water when young leaving his facial skin red and unevenly marked. It seemed to be his fate to suffer a lot of abuse, mostly from children, who just thought it funny to call him that name.

He was a very gentle sort and he would just go off sulking somewhere. It was that way when Hanny and I spotted him, leaning over a gate to a field, but as we looked at him he started shaking his huge fists. Unsure of what to do, Hanny got off her bike and approached him, to ask if he was all right. He pointed to his feet and studied them for a while. He'd taken off his boots, and his socks were saturated with the wet mud he was standing in. Suddenly he spotted me and pointed at my soft leather high lace up boots. He looked at them for a long time and then, in a very distorted and muffled voice boomed, "That's what oi wants, lovely boots like 'Eee." I promptly tried to hide my feet; he wasn't going to get mine.

Hanny and I left him, agreeing that he sure needed new boots. We heard him muttering to himself as we peddled away. We told Mum when we got back and the next Sunday we saw him in the Salvation Army, in the back row. Mum and I went over to see him.

He proudly showed us his new boots. "Oi loves these boots," he said. "Me feet did 'urt in t'other uns and oi couldn't run away fast, when they teases me. The Salvation Army gave me these new uns."

Spring Cleaning

"Hold on tight, Mien," Mum said, as I was on top of the rickety raggedy stepladder. "I'm sending up the suds later, first pass down the china." The Elephant teapot first, then the flowery vase, Grandma's pretty fruit bowl next, then the coffee can, so tall, glasses, and other lovely porcelain pieces were passed down.

"That is all now, Mien, so here is the bucket with suds, try to wring out the rag as tight as you can, before you wipe off the shelving there." And now the ceiling, which had gone so yellowy brown from the fire.

The rickety wooden ladder was placed all around the walls of the big room, to clean every bit of shelf and ceiling, after which all the lovely ornaments were placed back onto the shelves again. Hanny usually then cleaned the middle of the ceiling when she was home. The carpets were taken outside to be beaten mercilessly with the **mattenklopper** (willow carpet beater).

The curtains were washed and for that we had the first manual washing machine, which I believe Dad invented. It was constructed of a large empty wine barrel, sown in half with two wooden stompers in it, which were set onto a wooden cogwheel, and all of that was attached to a handlebar sticking out of the barrel on one side.

We had to wind the handle in turns as it was very hard to do, but it would stamp the wooden feet things up and down to agitate the clothes and suds and too often (unfortunately) also pulverized the buttons and clips.

It was a yearly spring clean operation and when it was all finished it looked beautiful. Mum usually then bought a small flowering plant, a primula or a French marigold, but Dad sometimes used to bring a hydrangea from the market.

The net curtains were always things of pride to all the housewives and, even if Mum was not unduly concerned with who had the whitest nets, she still made an effort to have them looking neat.

So these had to be washed by hand as they were much too delicate to stand the rigorous treatment of the wooden stompers. Carefully they were laid out to dry onto the small grass patch we had. Keeping an eye on them so they did not blow away.

I had just been sent to the corner shop to buy a pound of flour, and some dried prunes, with Freddy. Happily walking along I saw something flying in front of us. Freddy wanted to catch it and rag it to bits, when I spotted that it was one of our nets, oh how I tried to get hold of it.

Freddy was beside himself with mirth when he finally succeeded, making a dramatic jump for it, catching it with his sharp teeth.

"Give it here Freddy," I wailed. "Go on give, give, come on now, give." He pulled and I strained and it tore in half like a bit of paper. He shook his head dragging it through the mud.

Oh it was just a rag now. How dreadful, what are we going to tell Mum now? You naughty dog. Mum came running out of the gate just then and I ran on to tell but Freddy was much faster, he ran over the nets which were still spread over the grass with his muddy paws. This was a disaster.

That week, one of the windows was bare but Mum was busy on her sewing machine and I noticed that we had a really neat new curtain, which I thought I had seen before somewhere. Only it was pink. Did Mum have a nightie like that?

The Girl Who Saw Too Much

Lieve Papa en Rien   **10 July 1941**

Mama is helping me with this letter, as I am not yet able to write properly. I have to leave the little kinder garden school now; I am getting too big for that. Mama says I am a big girl now and I will have to go to the big school, we went to see the head teacher Mr Hamerlink, he says I can go into first form, it sounds too grand Papa, but I will have a nice teacher called Juffrouw Tillink, I will be able to write better then.

It is so warm outside and I get very hot, Mama says I am like a little tin saucepan, soon too hot and soon too cool, I wish you were here to push me on my swing.

When are you coming back Papa? We all miss you so much, Kisses from me, Mientje.

Helmi Wolff

At Last, Big School

You are big enough now to go to big school, I was told. It was not a bit like the preschool I had enjoyed on alternative days. I was not used to the rough games and the resentful treatment of some of the children. I was rubbish at sports; my foot would not let me run hard without tripping up. I tried hard but could not catch ball or skip a rope although I became better at that as I grew. I hated having to wear the especially made to measure high lace up boots, to accommodate and train my left foot to grow straighter.

Mrs Tilling was lovely and I learned well, knowing already quite a lot of the alphabet and being able to do simple sums. She was my favourite teacher particularly because she did a lot of art, beautiful drawings on the black board with real coloured chalks for us to copy, or in the case of nature studies, to learn from.

She praised me on my imaginative drawing once and that made me try even harder, but I knew I'd cop it later, to be called teacher's pet. If only I was not so sensitive and could dismiss it like nonsense. Lientje called it crap, but that was rude I knew. So the next time she praised me I felt forced to scratch over the top of the drawing to avoid intimidation.

At play times I tried desperately to be one of them. I ran and tripped at pointers until my lungs ached but I was no hero and I often wished for the ground to swallow me up when I failed so miserably. It became a source for being left out and even despised; I was picked on mercilessly.

One very tall girl called Tieny, whose father was the town's photographer, started to chase me after school time, as she was going almost the same way home. Of course with her long legs she was easily able to catch me, and when she did, she would punch and kick me, helped by her hero friend Tillie. I tried to hide in alcoves of shops or little alleyways, but she always saw me.

Yet again I was kicked on my painful foot, supposedly by accident with a snide remark like, "Oh, did that hurt, Mientje?"

I was still excluded from their games, which was hard to bear for me; I often felt very lonely and was scared of home time in case I got targeted. I literally started shaking when we were standing next to our desks in an orderly fashion to go home.

One day when I came home with cuts and bruises, Mum tried to console me. She put some fat and brown paper on the wounds, tied it down with some cotton strips that doubled at night times for **palviottes**, 'hair curlers', and said, "When I have cooked the dinner we are going to Tieny's parents' shop. I want them to see what has been done to you, this cannot go on."

I was scared stiff in case I'd be even more of a target, but I need not have worried, Tieny's mother was appalled at what her daughter had done when she saw my injuries. Tieny never actually chased me again but she stayed nasty in other ways to me.

Lientje van Dam and I became good friends. She was also a bit of a loner like me and we understood each other, we stayed friends throughout our school years.

Later in the third year, Mrs Zuidemar was our teacher, she had taught both my sister and brother before me, and for some reason did not like me a lot. Once she said to me, "Why can't you be like them, more cheerful?" I did not realize how serious I seemed to her.

It was the day of the exam in arithmetic. I was quite good at that, but Lientje could not keep up the speed. I tried to show her my paper with the answers, but we were caught, the punishment being, having to stand at the back of the class facing the wall with the proverbial dunce's cap on.

Helmi Wolff

By then because of malnutrition and other shortcomings and in Lientje's case also neglect, we both had a bladder infection. Unable to hold on to relieve ourselves, both of us put up our hand in the air, shuffling madly, but we were not allowed to go to the toilets, and the urine started leaking and running down our legs. I started to cry but Lientje whispered, "Don't, just don't, don't let them see your tears."

"But we're not allowed to pee and it hurts," so we just had to wet ourselves and be made fun of by the other kids.

First we were ignored, I dared to ask to be excused, but was told to stay still, at which everyone sniggered, they knew we could not stand still. The punishment for that was that we had to ask the cleaner for a mop and some cloths to mop up our spill, in front of the class.

Lientje seemed to be more hardened to this harsh treatment and she was not picked on as much as me because she could ignore teasing.

One teacher I sort of fell in love with, was Mr van Rossun. He taught fifth form and I was eight by then. He was kind, charming and good looking, and sensitive to all the needs of his class. He had observed the teasing and tried to avoid it all round. When the school bell rang, he'd ask me to stay on for an extra lesson or correcting off my homework.

"So Mientje," he said, "how will you get home?"

"I run, Master."

"Well if you like, hop on the back carrier of my bike and I'll take you to the top of the Bartels weg." He also told me that he had nine children at home, wow I thought, they are so lucky to have a ready-made group to play with.

Helmi Wolff

Lieve papa en Rien 1942

Hanny made a doll for my birthday, she said the last one is too dirty and you can't get the smell out of it even after we washed it.

She made this new one in pink and dressed it in bits of her pretty house coat and some lace off her pretty blouse, it is so pretty, Papa. I call her Greta after my little friend at school, because she has black hair like the black wool Hanny made it with.

She also made a little bodice of pink silk for me with a lacy edge to it; I love the feel of the soft material. Frans made my tricycle bigger because I have grown taller now, he had to put the saddle higher and the pedals bigger and he painted it a nice blue all over. Mama has tied some lovely red ribbons on to the handlebars, and my chair was decorated lovely for my birthday.

Have you got enough to eat, Papa?

Mama made sauerkraut with a sausage Frans got from the farmers.

I wished we could see you soon, then you could take us to the seaside, and Aunt Anna, I liked her.

Love and kisses Mientje

The Girl Who Saw Too Much

My lovely niece and nephews, and Dubbie Dog.

Helmi Wolff

Bath Time and Small Bedrooms

Saturday evening was bath time for us all, to get us cleaned up ready for church in the morning. Mother boiled pan and kettle in the hearth, and the range, to fill a tin bath, in front of the warm fire in the sitting-cum-dining room. This mammoth task was done straight after supper.

Still, it must have been even more of an upheaval when my three eldest sisters Fransien, Wijna and Nelly plus brother Rien were still at home.

All the week's washing was on the floor, sheets and towels, mainly for us to dry ourselves on, and getting the last use out of them, before the great washing day on Monday.

"Mien, you're first, it's nice and warm," Mum said. Oh, I'd been waiting, to sit in the lovely warm water. Normally green soap was used for washing and shampooing but if it got into your eyes it stung like billy-o. Dad had worked for the *'klock soap'* factory, equivalent of Sunlight soap, and the last of the precious bar was used for me. Even then a little stinging had to be endured, while my hair was given a hearty rubbing, but Mum said, "You are a big girl now, Mien," yes and the sooner it was rinsed off with the enamel mug the happier I'd be.

Next was Frans, he managed it all by himself and not a drop of water spilled on the washing when he draped the biggest sheet around him and made horrible gnashing noises to frighten everyone and pretend he was a ghost, ah but I knew it was him. Mum started to sing some lovely old song, one which I knew, and I tuned in as well.

The Girl Who Saw Too Much

Hanny was next. Mother insisted on privacy for us all, so I was given some paper and crayons to draw in the meantime, but I still noticed that Hanny had lovely little breasts starting to grow. I asked Mum about that, but she said, "We don't talk about that now, but when you are her age you will get some too."

Ever after that I used to check if they had grown a bit, but I was a late developer, and even at the age of fifteen, I had still not got much up top there. In fact when a girl friend called Anneke jokingly said to me, "What are we going to do with you then like two peas on a plank?" Gosh, I thought it shows and I started to wear Hanny's brassier stuffed with some soft silk stockings.

But bath time was over and Mum walked me up the stairs in my clean nightie, singing a ditty, which would coincide with each tread of the steps.

1,2 kopje tee
3,4 glaasje bier
5,6 kurk op de fles
7,8 soldaat op wacht
9,10 Roselien, laat je rooie rokje zien.

In English;

1, 2, cup of tea,
3, 4, glass of beer,
5, 6, cork on the bottle,
7, 8, soldiers marching,
9, 10, Roselyn show your pretty skirt.

Well by that time, if I had not reached the top of the stairs yet, a firm patting on my bum would begin, and I'd squeal with excitement, running to my bed, where a boisterous rumble, *rat, tat, tat, tat,* on my bum, like a drum, followed.

Finally in bed, it was song time. I could always choose which one she should sing for me; invariably I chose the entire children's operetta of the play garden. It was the longest and liveliest, and I still remember every verse of it now.

Last of all a short prayer also in song form was sung by us both, if I was not already asleep by then.

Four small bedrooms under the eaves of the roof were insulated with wooden planks directly adjoining the tiled roof under the eaves; consequently they were very warm in summer and freezing cold in the winter. Every noise outside and inside seemed to be magnified to me.

I had a particular abhorrence for the hooting steam trains, some streets away where at the station they would stand hissing and screeching like the evil dragon we had learned about at school. I had to bury my head under the pillow and crawl down further into the bedclothes, to shut out the noise.

I didn't want to cry, but Mum knew my fear, and the resulting nightmares. She would come up to see if I was distressed, then we would sing a lovely little prayer together to stop the noise, and it always worked.

The Girl Who Saw Too Much

The house, 56 Bartelsweg, as it is now.

Helmi Wolff

Our Classroom

"Mientje, go and get a new chalk from the Headmaster," said Mrs Radema our teacher in the third class.

"Oh yes, Miss, I will," I said. After getting up with a straight back and standing momentarily next to my desk, as was the requirement, I speeded off to do the important task. I had to negotiate the long corridor which took me past a few corners, and at one blind spot a door flew open, I had no time to stop in time, the door banged hard on to my forehead. *Bang*! It almost knocked me out I fell and reeled to get up again. I looked about but no one was in sight, whoever threw the door at me did not stop to see; perhaps whoever it was never knew.

I stood there swaying and dizzy, seeing fireworks splattering around my head. What was it I had to do? Ah yes, get a chalk for the teacher to write with on the blackboard. Which way now? I was on a mission to the Headmaster, straight on I went, arriving at the right door now, I knocked and was let in. Mr Hamerlink took one look at me and saw me still reeling like a drunken person. He must have seen the huge bump on my head, asking what happened, he sent me straight home. I couldn't find my way back home immediately, but a neighbour saw me, and took me home to Mum.

She was shocked to see the bump, and me, but what I was most upset about was, that I never completed my important mission.

Another sad incident in the class concerned my friend Lientje. She was left-handed, when writing, which was not allowed, and although she tried her best to write with her right hand, her words and spelling looked like scrawling. It was not legible and never fitted neatly between the lines. Consequently she was smacked on her hands and over the knuckles with a ruler so many times, that the blue and red bruises were severe, and she would suck them for comfort, which again furthered an attack on her.

She was determined not to cry, she said in her family there were worse things happening but she would not be a cry baby. I did admire her for that, and she taught me to do the same.

"Don't cry," she told me, "just don't."

"You are in detention," said my teacher for not keeping your arms neatly folded and hands above the desk, during the lesson. "After school you go to the top class, while you sit there you are to write your lines one hundred times." Yes Miss.

Whilst sitting there and writing away, some older boys came in and two of them came to sit either side of me. They were going to have a bit of fun with me.

"You ever had an injection, kid?" one asked me.

A very small "no," from me made him grin in an evil sort of way.

"Ah no," said one of the other boys, but he was eager to inflict some pain.

"See here this new fountain pen kid? This is a magic injection! So hold out your hand."

"No," I cried, but he grabbed it.

"Palm upwards, kid! And keep still." I pulled and kicked and screamed but no one else moved. "You will turn blue when I stick this in you and disperse the ink."

Petrified and struggling with him, the others got hold of me and pinned me down; it was gruesomely painful.

Screaming with pain and horror, scared to death, I escaped and ran, blindly ran and ran, till the stars in front of my eyes and tears blinded me.

When finally I got home, Mum was horrified at what had happened. She immediately started to suck out the ink and spat it out several times after which she took me to the doctor who put my arm into a sling to try to prevent blood poisoning, but to no avail. It took weeks with my arm in a sling for the swelling to subside.

That evening Mum and Hanny went to see the Headmaster with me in tow, to show the extent of the cruelty and damage that had been done. I think the boys concerned were identified and punished, especially the one that administered the ink injection.

My brother Frans asked me, in a sort of comical way, "And did you finish your lines, Mien? Or do I have to help you again?" Well never mind what I told him then.

I thought of Lientje and tried not to cry, remembering how she was caught looking at the answers on my page of arithmetic. We were often excluded from children's games.

Both of us wore hand-me-downs in the war, coupons were scarce and kids can be oh so cruel about your clothes at school.

I was on my own in the playground after school to swing on the play swings, when suddenly about ten kids surrounded me and bound me fast on a bench with skipping ropes. I struggled and screamed but to no avail and when I was tied up good, they started to tickle me all together furiously. It was terrible. I squirmed and cut my wrists on the rope to try to free myself. They would not stop and I felt myself lose consciousness. All I saw was a teacher trying to un-knot the ropes. The kids had scarpered.

When the tallest girl of our class said, "You can be our end girl in Slingertje," I was so chuffed.

"Yes please," I said.

"Well hold hands right at the end then." Fifteen kids held hands, the front girl began to run fast everyone ran as well, when suddenly she stopped with a jerk and of course the end of the Slinger went up in the air. I held on for grim life itself whilst flying through the air, before being thrown down on the ground again. We did it several times; it was really exhilarating to fly, even though it was very dangerous.

My stockings had holes on the knees, and my knees themselves had quite nasty and bloody scrapes. Mum looked at the damage, and said, "You can't ruin your stockings fast enough can you, Mien? I got those for you with the last coupons only a few weeks ago!"

Ah I felt in that time spell, in the grip of a cruel war. Life seemed cheaper than clothes. It was a big worry as to where to get the next pair of stockings from, especially those woolly ones that I ruined. People on the whole were more concerned with material things such as clothing and shoes, which were so hard to come by.

It was often said that if you had a nasty scratch or bite or sting, "Oh that will heal by itself, but the tear in your clothes won't."

I think this reflected in the children, they would really be more upset about muddy shoes or a torn garment, than any little injury on themselves.

Helmi Wolff

My Beautiful Pear Tree, Snakes and Nightingales

That spring the pear tree was absolutely beautiful, its white blossoms covering every little branch like frothy white lace.

I loved it so much, visualising a picture I'd seen of a bride in her lovely pure white lace gown.

We had an old box camera, which came out very seldom, but now an exception was made and Mum took a photo of that gorgeous tree. When it was developed almost a year later, in black and white, we put it in a little frame that Hanny had made of coloured cardboard and some ribbon.

A great show of pears was expected. The bees had zoomed merrily around the blossom all spring, and soon we saw the forms of small pears.

I never quite knew what kind they were, perhaps Sweet-Williams or Conference, but they were enormous, so sweet and juicy.

I couldn't wait to sink my teeth into one.

When they finally started to change colour, I spotted one that looked ripe enough to eat.

"Frans, can you reach that one please?" I asked glowing with the effort of trying to reach one myself.

"Well," he drawled, "Have you tidied and cleaned your room, Mien?" Oh bother.

"No not today."

"I'll pick a few, and keep yours here for later then." It was well worth the cost, and it didn't take that long anyway, but my mouth was dribbling with anticipation.

The Girl Who Saw Too Much

That whole early part of the summer, we gorged on the juicy pears, and Mum made so many pear pancakes, or stewed with some pap.

I even took one to school, for playtime, and tried unseen by the others to give one to the teacher, who also enjoyed the juicy fruit.

Finally when autumn came, they started to fall, some smashed down to break into pieces on the stones below. Mother had an idea, but first…

"Oh, they taste so good," we said when Vickie and I were gathering them up, "A shame some of them are so smashed, we could get all the kids from the block here to have a feast," we fantasized.

"Yah," said Vicky, "they would all have the runs tomorrow, and have a day off from school."

I couldn't quite see the logic of that assumption, but still I suppose she knew what she meant.

Mum came out.

"Mien, get the wheelbarrow and spade, go to Sprenge (spring) woods, and get some heather to spread under the tree."

"That sounds like fun," Vickie said, trying to push the heavy old barrow made of solid worn out wood. This barrow had been in the shed ever since I can remember.

Feeling quite important holding the spade over my shoulder like I'd seen Frans do when he had to take it to his friend Henkie, and whistling to the tune of 'Onward Christian Soldiers', I set off with Vickie. We were on an adventure; it was very exciting.

"Here or there?" asked Vickie, meaning where do we enter these woods. 'Easy peasy'.

"The nearest end, adjoining the Juliana Hospital." We had to push the barrow together through the heavy soil of the woods, but soon we saw what we were looking for – great looking heather and lots of it. It was my turn to dig, but as soon as I dug the spade in, something moved quite violently.

A snake, in fact a whole nest of snakes, wriggling and rearing up at us. **"Aaaarrrgghh!"** we yelled and screamed, running away as fast as we could, never mind about the spade and barrow.

We were so startled and scared when we arrived back home, that Mum had a job calming us down. "So," she asked, "where are the tools now?"

Just then we heard Frans coming home and ran to tell him the story. "We'd better go and see about it," he said, adding, "Girls are sissies."

"Well," started my friend, defending herself. I threw her a look that said, 'Not now, Vickie'. We knew we shouldn't have left the spade and barrow.

Trying to keep up with him on the pavements, we hurried behind him following along a short cut through someone's garden and across the railway line. "Don't you do this on your own," he warned us.

It was magic; we were at the woods already. Frans started running and we shouted after him, "No, not there, further in." And yes, there were the barrow and spade, just as we had left them.

We would not go near because of the snakes and we could hear the dreaded things hissing.

"Girls, huh!" said Frans as he started digging. In no time at all he filled the barrow with plaques of good spongy heather. He put the spade on top and asked us if we wanted a ride. We clambered on top of the soft heather and he ran all the way home pushing us.

Later that day, the girls from our newly formed little choir started to arrive at the back door.

Lientje was first. Atie and Biekie came together but Vickie said she would be late so we started without her.

Choir practice was a serious business. We decided that Tuesdays was the best day for it. Vickie and I had asked a few more girls we liked to join but they were not enthusiastic about practising in our back kitchen, even with a glass of water thrown in.

Mum's old treadle organ, like a harmonium, was there for us. I had organ lessons and hoped to use my skills to encourage the singers to harmonise. The other organ, the best one, was in the parlour. It was a lovely American silk wood antique, with a truer and smoother tone. You could pull out the stops to make it sound like a violin or a human voice and, as Mum was the church organist, she could really 'pull out all the stops'.

I accompanied the four-girl choir playing mostly with one finger but also managing a few chords.

Tapping the side of the organ with a smooth little stick to gain their attention.

On this afternoon, I prepared to wave my baton when Vickie came in.

The songbook we were using was a familiar one and we had chosen *The Day that the Balloon Went Up*.

To the tune of: *'Didn't we have a lovely day, the day we went to Bangor'*.

I struck a chord and all four tried to sing it. "No, no, no, try again, to hit the right notes."

I was hoping Mum would hear us, and come to the rescue, but that didn't happen. No luck there, I thought.

Still, they were good, if not a very determined bunch, and we got going, singing with one voice. Maybe we could start to harmonise a bit now I thought? Our ages ranged from seven to ten or so.

Tapping the side of the organ again, I sorted the altos from the sopranos and tried with my one finger effort to demonstrate the sound of the harmony. Mum came in and said, "I'll do that, Mien, while you get together with the girls." Fantastic, I thought. The response was really good, two and two, nicely all the way.

Mum asked what we called ourselves and we said we didn't have a name as yet, but yes, it would be nice to have a name now that we were in production.

'Four Singers' came up, but Biekie said she didn't like that.

"My dad is in a band called **'Fanfare'**," she said, "but that might be a bit grand."

'The Kitchen Singers' and *'The Young Girls'* were also mentioned, we 'ummed and ahhed'.

"What about *The Nightingales'?*" Mum said.

Yes, we all felt that this could be us, and also that it was the best name by far. We were feeling really proud of ourselves and after Mum left we tried the balloon song again and, although it was not good with my one finger accompaniment, it was not too bad either.

We had just got into the next song, a ditty about camping around the fireside, when the back door opened again and in came Frans, tired from sawing wood for a neighbour to earn the money for his bicycle tax disc for the year. To us *'Nightingales'*, it was an intrusion into the middle of our serious fun.

"Oh," said Frans. "The crows are crowing again."

Everyone stopped singing and said, "What did he call us?"

"Croak, croak, croak," he added as he passed through.

"Oh how dare he!" I said. "That is just like my bothersome brother."

The Nightingales' were not of long duration. We tried, unsuccessfully, to get more girls interested and we eventually drifted apart and disbanded.

Helmi Wolff

Hanny and Nelly, on the upstairs balcony.

The Girl Who Saw Too Much

Frans taught me guitar playing and I loved it.

Helmi Wolff

Another Washing Day

It was Lientje's turn to help her mum with the week's washing, "Oh she moaned I hate Mondays."

"Do you want to come home with me then?" I half-heartedly ventured, thinking she would surely not dare to shun her chores at home, but she jumped at it and I was thrilled to have her walk home with me.

We had both been in trouble at school about our dreaming, looking out of the window, and also for yelling at a boy, who kept pulling my plaited pigtails.

Lientje's hands looked sore, and she said that it made her hands bleed to rub and scrub at the washing, and her Mum always shouted at her for staining the sheets, while her brother was sarcastic and said things like, "Not much like the drifting snow huh?"

Why do girls always have to do everything, she sort of asked, boys get away with the lot, while they make the most mess and dirt!

I tried to sympathize and really found it hard to imagine why they were so hard on her, especially if she had to do it all in horrible soda suds.

Turning into our road, I could see everyone's washing flapping in the wind, some colourful and some greyish white; some people had spread their whites on the grass and hung over hedges.

Lientje trotted alongside of me in her very worn shoes, one with the entire sole missing. How did she manage to walk in them?

I'd been telling her, about the wonderful washing machine, Dad had made before he was taken away. "Well it is sort of an automatic clothes washer he made from a half wine barrel, with a handle sticking out, on one side, which turns two stompers up and down on to the washing, when you turn it. But it smashes any buttons so my Mum has sewn poppers and hooks on everything."

"Oh, ah," said Lientje, admiring our Dad's invention. "Me Mum could do with that," she said. "It makes her arms ache just to look at our dirty washing with nine kids!"

We reached the gate, and… there was our washing on the back line; it must have been Mum's last batch of washing rags, through the grey worn out suds.

"Ah," remarked Lientje, when she saw our sadly flapping sodden rags. "No soap then either huh? Ah just like ours then."

Helmi Wolff

A New Grand Bathhouse

The new bathhouse was a real boost for almost everyone in our village. It had always been a swimming pool and showers, but now a large part was converted into long corridors with small cubicles housing a bathtub in each one. The road was even called *'Bad weg'* (bath road).

"Ready, Mien?" Frans called.

"Yes I'm coming," I replied. We had to bring our own flannel, towel and soap.

"We don't need the bike, we can run it," Frans said. Of course Freddy wanted to come too.

"Later, boy," said Mum. That dog was so clever, he knew, drooping his tail with a big sigh, he returned to his basket and buried his nose.

We had to wait quite a while and, in the meantime, I was occupied looking at all the people who were also waiting in the queue. One man had such a baldhead, with lumps and bumps that it seemed like his face had grown over the top as well. How, I thought, does he know where his face ends?

It took quite a while, for the queue to lessen, but our turn came and we were both shown to our separate cubicles. The bath master showed me the hot tap, out of which a measured amount of water would flow. I marvelled that hot water would come out of a tap; I had only ever seen Mum having to heat water on the range or hearth, and then lift the heavy pan off, to pour the boiling water into the tin bath in front of the warm hearth.

The water was just the right temperature for me, as it gushed out of the tap, and I wondered if I had to turn it off again, and how would I know? I needn't have worried because it stopped all of a sudden; oh I hope I didn't break it.

"Don't be long," he said. "Otherwise your brother has to pay more!" Tentatively I stepped into the warm bath. It was lovely, and it made me feel comfortable all over, I was gloating and floating in the lovely warmth of the water, when suddenly I noticed something. I saw a dark stripe over my tummy, but when I went to rub it, I could wipe it away, and then I realized that it was a long hair, so nothing to worry about. What with the lovely warmth, I started to feel quite dreamy, instead of scrubbing up.

In no time at all, a loud knocking was heard on my door.

"Time's up, come on out now." Oh dear, I hadn't scrubbed up, my nails weren't clean yet. Frantically I tried, but there was a second knock at the door and Frans's voice saying, "Come on out, Mien, otherwise I have to pay more." I just got out of that lovely water, no time to even towel dry, but that didn't matter it was warm there anyway.

"I'm coming, I'm coming," I shouted back, desperately trying to dress before opening the door.

How did Frans manage to look so neat, with combed hair as well?

Helmi Wolff

Lieve papa en Rien   June 1942

Frans took me to 'Het Badhuis', it has lots of baths with hot water in tiny steamy rooms.

When I sat in the bath I did not want to come out, it was so lovely, but Frans knocked at the door and said, to come out quickly, otherwise he'd have to pay double money. I had to put my clothes on wet, there was no time to dry off, but it is so warm there that it didn't matter.

How are you and Rien, Papa? Can you get your favourite bread pap there? Mamma makes it for us in the morning and we get sugar beet syrup on it, that is yummy but I don't like the levertraan (cod liver oil).

It was wonderful to get your letter after we had to wait such a long time, Mama started marching and dancing around the table, we all did it and we clattered the spoons and forks together like a brass band, I'll draw it for you, we miss you so much kisses. Mientje

T h e   G i r l   W h o   S a w   T o o   M u c h

Helmi Wolff

Play Nurses

"When I grow up," I said, "I want to be a nurse, with a lovely cape, and a cap, and a pretty apron."
"Yes, let's play nurses, Vicky," I said again.
"Mum's gone out, and there are some freshly mangled sheets, pillow cases and tea towels in the linen cupboard, we could wrap and fold these around us, and fasten it with a safety pin, to look like a proper nurse's uniform."
"Let's draw a red cross with our wax crayons on two tea towels," Vicky proffered. "That looks real huh?"
After we fastened these round our heads, we felt ready to gather our patients, from around the block. We were not short of those, after we promised them a sugar pill, from Mum's little box she always seemed to have with her in church to keep me good and quiet.
At least Bieky, Atie, Henkie, Toon, Aafke and Leentje followed us to the promised makeshift hospital round the back of our house.
We took our whole entourage round, where the patio made a good place for a hospital; we borrowed the dining room's cushions, rags and fluffy dog blanket from Freddy's basket, to make beds for our many patients. It took some while to get them all to lie down and stop giggling, we were dead serious, and it all seemed so real to us.
"First," Vicky said, "we have to test you all, for your ears." We had seen that at school, one of the children was told at that time to get his Mum to wash behind his ears, as he was growing a moss

forest there. The poor kid was crying by the end, he thought the moss forest would eat him all up.

Another boy had an itchy ear and he was given some cream to take home for his mum to apply to his sore itchy ears, but curiosity and temptation got the better of him. After a while he took the lid off the little cardboard box and dipping in his finger, he first smelt it and then tasted it; a terrific howl ensued after which much coughing and choking, shouting, "Oi ain't goin' to get that on me here ear!"

One girl was told that she had wax in her ears. "That's funny," she said. "Mum uses wax for her wooden table, but I didn't know that she used it on me ears as well."

"Everybody on your sides now, so we can examine your ears," I shouted at random, "left first and then right." Vicky started one end and I the other.

"Not too deep," Leentje said.

"I am not even near your ear," I retaliated.

"We have to test your eyes next," and producing a little cup, I said, "You just rinse with it."

"When are we going to get our sugar pill," Biekie shouted.

"When we have given you your injections." That caused a bit of a stir.

"But first," I continued, "we have some lovely medicine for you all," as I scooped a teaspoon at a time out of the homemade lemonade jug to give to everyone, no need to ask them to swallow there!

Our patients seemed a little more settled after that, and quite willing to be prodded and poked about some more. "Is your back always so hot?" I asked Atie.

"I am cold not hot," Atie replied. "I don't have enough blankets."

"How come your left leg is bent?" I asked Aafke.

"It is not bent," she scowled indignantly. "It's where me Dad hit me." Horrified I looked again, it was blue and swollen, and so I did what my parents always did, if I had an injury.

I wet some white strips of cotton and bandaged her up. I think it hurt her a lot, but she tried not to winch. I thought she deserved another spoon of the lovely sweet liquid for being so brave, which started all the others whining for some more too. Oh well, why not, come to that, Vicky felt that we ourselves deserved some more. The jug was, by now, only half full and I rationed it out a bit, but; it tasted so good, and it was so thirst quenching.

"Any broken legs?" I shouted! No reply at all. "Oh come on now any one? It won't hurt, it is only pretend."

"Me sister broke her arm and it did hurt a lot," a small voice was heard to say.

Everything was going so well, until we said it was injection time. "Everyone turn over please." Vicky found a great big darning needle in the sewing basket, and out she came with it.

Alarmed every one sat up straight. "No, no, no!"

I went to take it out of her hand. "Much too big," said I with all the authority I could muster, getting a smaller but sharper and probably more vicious looking one, at which every patient got up as fast as they could and ran away.

"Why did you do that?" Vicky asked. "They liked my needle better!"

Playing Shops 1942

"Shall we play shops, Vicky?" I asked.

"We could use the empty shed at my house now," she replied.

Vicky lived in the next road, with her mum and Gran; the Gestapo had taken her father as well, to do hard labour in Germany, the same as my Dad and brother Rien. We did not need to walk round the block to get to her home, as her uncle the stone mason, who lived opposite us, bordered onto Vicky's garden.

They didn't mind us tripping through their ground and often called us in to give us a sweet. Mr and Mrs Boomgaard had one son. He was a big lad at fifteen, and I noticed that he was a bit slow, but nice. He had a gift for whistling and singing like a bird, in perfect tune and pitch, we often listened to him, and Mum sometimes played the organ in accompaniment.

At Vicky's place there was a lovely almost empty old shed, which was great for all sorts of things and for us to play in. This time it made a super shop with shelves and a table already there.

We had to take it in turns to be shopkeeper and customer.

Well talk about, 'open all hours' we literally invented it. It was quite a job getting everything organized, setting up the planks with little pots and pans; terracotta flower pots made great filters for the sand inside to flow though the centre hole.

We found different coloured sand which we took from the sand pit of Vicky's little brother Sam. He yelled as we took some of his precious little castle but we needed it to have pretend flour, salt and sugar.

Vicky produced a bag of beads, which were ideal for cherries on top of the mud cakes or gravel fruitcakes. Paper was very scarce, but we had saved some for shops. We giggled a lot as we tried to fold the bits of paper and make them sand proof and leak proof.

"Oh," I said. "You are hopeless at this, Vicky, I'll make them, because I've been to a proper big school for this, so leave it to me."
Bossy boots!

Someone was shouting, we could hear it coming from the outdoor loo. "What happened to the paper I just hung on the hook? How am I going to wipe my bum now, I bet those kids have been at it!"

"Well," came the reply from inside the house. "You'll have to wait now, I've nearly finished reading the paper, and then I'll tear it into bits for yer!"

Vicky was the first customer. "One pound of sugar please." I weighed it on a little plank balanced and suspended on a ridged stone, with different sized smaller graded stones on one side, and the goods to be weighed on the other side.

It actually worked of a sort. "Anything else, Mrs van Klomp?"

"Yes, a piece of cake please."

Now that was tricky, as the mud cake crumbled, but I gave her a bit extra for good measure.

So now it was my turn. "Some salt please, a small bag will do."

"Oh dear I'm afraid we're out of salt," came the reply, and no amount of winking and blinking on my part in the direction of the lighter sand would convince her to give me that, but she had an idea, a brainwave surely, as she said, "Wait a minute."

I could not believe my eyes when she walked over to the canary's cage, and opening the little door she crushed the minute big jobs at the bottom of its tray with her fingers to make a little fine white powder, which was put in the little bag she was already holding. "Anything else?"

The Girl Who Saw Too Much

"Oh no, thanks."

So now we change over again, and she says, "Half a pound of brown beans please," as she comes through the shed door.

A bit of inventive thinking as I replied, "Wait a minute," and walking over to the rabbit cage, I carefully opened the little door not to let 'Sneeuwtje' (Snowy) escape.

I gathered a hand full of wet black bumbles, put them in a bag, folded them over especially slowly to add importance to this miracle, and said, "Here you are, that will be two cents."

The bag of round wet bumbles was handed over, and taken with suitable importance for such a speciality, so she left to walk up the garden path.

Suddenly the bag broke and because she was holding it so close to her, the lovely silky yellow dress she was wearing got badly stained.

"Who's done that?" came her Mum's voice.

"Mientje," said Vicky. Her mother was not well pleased, and she said so.

The consequence was that I had to stay away from her house for a week. Still, Vicky came to our house every day. And that was really necessary to keep our saga play up to date as it had got left behind with all the other play stuff.

We had also made a dolls house with the help of a cardboard box on its side. Windows and a door were cut out of the sides. Mum gave us some pretty paper to stick on to the inside for wallpaper, stuck with stiffly made starch which was left from the washing. Some tiny pictures were cut out of papers, and frames were crayoned around them, which served as decoration.

We had made cosy cardboard chairs and a table, even a matchbox settee took up one of the sides.

Mrs Stemerdink gave me a little piece of red velvet with which we covered all the furniture and floor space.

This homemade dolls house had a paper cut-out people-family living in it. Whole family sagas were enacted in there. Every day we imagined new problems or outings or anything we had gleaned from the grown-ups, such as little Keesie had to be taken to hospital, or naughty Klaas had not been at school and got found out. We played bed times, waking up and cleaning the house after the children etc.

It amused us for hours on end, the father had to go to work; dinner time, berry picking, cooking, going to church in their Sunday best using the front room for Sundays only and for visitors, we even planned a holiday to a warm land.

Everyone had to be redressed into cotton clothes for that, which we cut out from a magazine the dressmaker lady gave us. Sometimes we had to draw, colour and paint the clothes ourselves before cutting them out.

The thrill of hanging them onto the paper people was so real.

Hours of imaginative play kept us happy. Did Josey take her medicines? Oh no? She doesn't like it? What about Theo's cod liver oil? We will have to disguise it with some jam, what no jam? Well – boiled beetroot juice then, if we don't have anything else.

The Girl Who Saw Too Much

Fun and Games (A)

One game that I enjoyed a lot was *'Tollen'*, (spinning top). I had become very good at this and was able to keep my wooden spinning top going by skilfully applying the sweep to just give the top enough spin to coax it over the rough bumps in the crude sand roads.

It became a competitive game, to be able to keep it going without stopping all the way from home to school. I had claimed twice now that I had done this, but of course this had to be seen to be believed; so it was arranged that Eefje and Geertje should accompany me home to see if I would have to stop anywhere.

They were to walk either side of me, while I spun the top continuously until I got to my home. That is easier said than done, as to go home was up hill very slightly, and if I encountered any obstacles the force of the sweep had to be applied with more gusto. "Well don't be in my way then," I said, "because if you are, it won't count if it stops." They were quite nice girls, and we set out to try.

On the pavement I was doing well even over the undulating slabs of it, but now I had to go on the road, in the grit and sand. Skilfully I made my top spin and jump onto the right spot in the road. I could feel the appreciation of the girls.

On I went over the middle of some of the small country ways, through alleys and on the sides of hedgerows. I was beginning to get quite smug, almost showing off now, I asked, "What about that hump you want me to go up, and over that?"

The hump was in someone's driveway but the gate was open, and encouraged by my success and the two admirers who had not got in my way so far, I started to go up and up. Just then a cat was disturbed by my friends, and the spinning thing ascending towards it, with a great maw-wow and a hiss, the cat sprung forwards right into the spinning path. Shocked, I lost my concentration, faltered, and the top spun out of control, down the drive towards the house.

We all got a bit of a fright. Which one of us was going to ask at the house to be allowed to retrieve my precious spinning top? We looked at each other, but the vote came down firmly on me.

"Well it is yours," said Geertje.

Yes too true, so! KNOCKING on the door, I heard no reply and saw no one. Suddenly the top window opened and a lady asked, "What do you want?"

"I've lost my Toll in your garden, could I please find it?"

"What!" she shouted back. "Speak up girl," she said again.

I didn't win the tournament this time, but still got a bit more respect from some of the girls, who were told by Geertje and Eefje that I almost did it.

Fun and Games (B)

Lientje and I got very good at a game called *'Hinkelen'*
We drew our various complicated patterns in the loose sand road; Lientje eyed it critically and observed a little crinkle in the straight line, where I had to avoid a small stone. "How do you think," she remarked, "I can jump accurately when I don't know where the line is?"
"Alright then clever clogs, you do it." She actually spat on the stone to see precisely where it had to go. Oh boy this is going to be a serious game!
We took turns hopping on one foot, round each course, without straddling the lines.
"That's a photo finish," she shouted. A what? No one had a magic camera in our neighbourhood except for the one little brownie box Mum had, and I knew for sure that she would never waste a picture on such a kid's game. "You touched the roundabout."
"No I didn't."
"What about this one then," and so on, but we stayed friends, in the end we didn't fall out over those things.
"You have to do the whole course without touching the lines, in the shortest possible time, and I was the quickest," she reiterated. NO, No! The only trouble was when the other kids wanted to join in. "You know," Lientje stated, "they are quicker messing up our patterns than we can draw them in again." Ah yes, that made us the friends we were.

Helmi Wolff

The Girl Who Saw Too Much

My hero brother, Frans, in scout's uniform, holding his bugle.

Helmi Wolff

The Windmill and Doggy Fun

It took a long time, standing in the queue with Frans at the windmill on the outskirts of Apeldoorn. It was hard to just stand still and wait for the great bottom doors to open.

The word had got around that the miller, Frits Vorderman, would rather give his corn and wheat away than be raided by the regular occurring raids with which the German soldiers kept interrupting his day. It was amazing how quickly the news got round, to get there on the double, to be dished out a small bag of grain each.

Mientje had her own plan once inside the mill, but before all that, she waited in the queue scoffing her feet to repeated demands from her brother to *"Stand still, Mien."*

There in front of them all were two doggies giving each other a piggyback.

Oh boy, having never witnessed anything like that before, I was amazed and full of admiration.

"Oh look Frans, oh look Frans, isn't that clever, oh I think that's so sweet, look, look, Frans look."

"Be quiet, Mientje," came the highly embarrassed reply from my teenaged brother. "Be quiet and don't look," he said. Not understanding his disinterest, and calling even louder.

"But *look* Frans these two doggies, *look*."

"Please shut up, Mientje," came the reply from the by now red in the face Frans, exasperated by the determination of his little sister he was responsible for.

Pulling her hand sharply upwards, causing a totally surprised, "Let go, don't do that."

By now everyone in the queue was laughing and pointing at the two totally undeterred dogs doing their thing, when suddenly right in the top of the mill a tiny window opened, and a bucket of water was thrown over the two offending dogs, perhaps by the miller's wife who looked most pleased with herself 'having reached her target'.

With loud yells and growls the dogs suddenly separated and stood bucking and weaving on the pavement, before running like the clappers. That floor show over, the great doors opened to the relief of all, still laughing and chuckling as they surged forward.

Everyone took turns to go in, and after a while, to reappear smiling with a bag of flour and grain. Our turn came. "Well, young man, what would you like?" asked Frits.

"One bag of flour and one of oats please."

The miller looked at me and said, "And you, young lady?"

"Some soup please sir."

"Ah well, just help yourself, any of these bags here will do." My little hands grappled in the corn, wheat, barley and any grain, filling my pockets to over flowing.

Later when Frans got on his bike, which never left his side, he lifted me onto the cross bar. "Here, Mien, hold these bags while we get home." I had a job to hold on to everything, whilst balancing on the cross bar of the speeding bike, holding my pockets too, so they would not spill any of the precious grain, whilst somehow holding on with my elbows and knees to stay on the wobbly bike.

We arrived at last, home was in sight. "Jump off," said Frans. Ah, easier said than done, my legs had gone to sleep, they buckled right under me when I hit the grit, very few grains actually got spilled as Frans had already taken the two big bags from me.

In the kitchen, Mum listened to my tale of two lovely doggies, and the bucket of water. "But Frans didn't see it Mum." A little smile crossed her face.

"Oh well, I have got soup," I said, and promptly turned out my pockets into a big enamel bowl. "So anyway," I announced, "we can have soup tonight," feeling important. "See Mr Frits gave me all the soup stuff for our supper, see?"

My lifelong friend, Gerry Vorderman, daughter of Frits the miller, remembers countless times, that he opened the doors to the public to help the starving people. Many stories came to light, such as her father hiding men in the mill to great danger of himself, and how the stance of the sails of the mill had a secret language of danger, or: 'come here', or, 'stay away' etc.

The Girl Who Saw Too Much

Lieve Papa en Rien   September 1943

Frans and I got some soup grains from that big windmill at the canal, the miller man said I could fill my pockets with oats and any corn I needed, Frans got some bigger bags with flour and oats

Mama was so happy about that we had delicious soup that night but Frans did not see the two doggies having a piggy back, they were so sweet, and the miller's wife threw a bucket with cold water out of the top window over them so they stopped, I'll draw it for you.

Love and kisses Mientje

A point recording here in reference is that this was forever after called the doggie soup day.

Helmi Wolff

1943 I loved my L, P + R, Frans + I got some Soup oranges from a Windmill by the canal, the miller man said I could fill my pockets with oats and corn, and anything else I could see. Hans got some bigger bags with flour Mamma was so happy about that, but Hans did not see two doggies having a piggyback, they were so sweet, but the miller's wife threw a bucket of cold water out of the top window over them, so they stopped. We had lovely soup last night mamma made it nice + thick, I love you Daddy + R. Mientje

windmill   *doggies*   *Soup*

21 Nov 44 L. P + R, yesterday was Mamma's birthday, Done. I made some lovely paper roses and Frans used his kite ribbons + Hanny had a pretty hair clip, to decorate her chair, before she got up, she was so surprised, and when she sat at it, she said, Now I feel like a proper Princess. She had her best blouse + skirt on, you know blue with yellow squiggles + flowers. I found a nice piece of wood, + Frans helped me to make an Easter Cross for her, she said she likes to putt that next to the photo's in her bedroom. Hanny gave her the hair clip, but she said "it is so lovely, that we should both wear it," so it looked nice on her hair at the back yesterday, but today Hanny is wearing it on the front of her hair. We had hutspot with carrots + onions for dinner. Do you get that there Papa? I expect you are too busy to come back to us? Lots of love Mientje x x

my blouse
hair clip
m. chair
Easter cross
huts pot

The Girl Who Saw Too Much

Helmi Wolff

Growing Veggies

"They're up," Mum called in astonishment, "green look, they're up, through the soil," and they were.

The first little leaves were showing.

These are the seeds from Mrs Freedenoord's garden, I concluded.

"Oh lovely, make sure you water them very gently, oh so carefully, Mien. They are so young yet and we don't want to wash them out of the soil eh?"

Even more amazing to us was that after a few days of careful nurturing they started showing red little globes. Radishes, we shouted together.

We had never grown things from seeds before.

Mum was so enthusiastic; she started collecting seeds from neighbours' gardens, who were pleased to give us some.

Soon small lettuce leaves and spinach rows popped up.

"Help me get these sticks in the ground, nicely in a row and crossed at the top."

The runner beans started to grow tall, and every morning I curled the new little tops round the sticks where they climbed up. It never ceased to surprise me how tiny red flowers turned into beans, which grew so long, we had to cut them in bits before cooking. Any left over, were picked for winter pickling.

The garden although small, became a great source of food for us, and we were proud to give some away to neighbours who in turn gave us some of their produce.

The Girl Who Saw Too Much

Lieve Papa en Rien   **Spring 1942**

Dear Daddy & Rien,

We are growing leaves from seeds. Mum sowed some tiny ones into the ground, and today they are up through the soil, showing little green leaves. I am watering them with the used water.

Mum says that the seeds swell up and start to eat and drink, isn't that amazing?

How are you, Papa, are you working hard with your lorry, and is Rien sawing wood?

Frans has sawn a pile of wood and cut some kindling too, to glow in the range.

I will tell you when we can eat the leaves and what they taste like a lot later when they have grown.

We miss you so much. Please write to us, kisses Mientje.xxxx

Helmi Wolff

Hanny in her self-made pretty dress,
in front of 56 Bartelsweg, our home.

Looking After Freddy

Frans had progressed a lot at his school, and he was accepted for the *'Mulo'* in Apeldoorn, which was like high school. The system for schooling was different to what it is now, e.g. at six years of age one went to 'Big school' (like primary school), until fourteen years of age so it would become Secondary and Grammar later, if a class had to be attended for a second time than the school leaving age became fifteen years of age. After which a pupil would go to *'Ambachts School'* [technical college] to learn a proper trade, or if the pupil was more academically minded, Mulo, or H. B. S. *(Hoge Burger School).*

Frans was bright, we were proud of him, he made the grade; he had to work hard at his homework, especially to start with.

The evenings were not long enough to do it all. I remember Mum calling up often, "Lights out now, Frans."

"Yes," he'd say. "In a minute," but I could see the small glimmer of light under his door long after. It was then that I made up my mind **not** to go to that kind of Grammar school, it was too much work.

At home I was given more responsible jobs now, and at eight years of age I was put in charge of making sure that our little dog *Freddy Fry*, (called after a famous radio reporter), was kept clean and flea free.

To that end I had to wash him weekly in lukewarm water in which was put the merest lick of green soap. It meant that I had to stop whatever I was doing, to clean him if he had dirty or greasy paws or sticky fur, to see to lovely Freddy, who hated getting wet but endured it, whilst I plied him with much cooing and little love words in the softest lilt I could muster. After which he would race upstairs, and if anyone had left the door open for him, he'd run in to get away from me and shake like anything, to get the water of him.

He was otherwise very pleasing and it was a treat to see him curl up in his clean rag basket, which had also been lined with clean paper first if we had it. I always made sure he had his favourite old slipper which he would stuff into my hands, to give him a game of tug, pull and shake, to test his strength, of course he always won.

It was surprising the stamina I had too, when we were playing, the pair of us thoroughly enjoying ourselves, having such a lot of fun in our rough and tumble. He was a super little character (a Heinz 57 varieties), such a constant companion and so loyal and loving. Especially when I was ill, when he was allowed upstairs, to lie so close to me, he made me feel better, and it was as if he knew when I was sad.

He would lay his little head on my hands or lap as if to say, 'I'm here, don't cry,' whilst he gave me a lick.

Sometimes we would all go to the woods. He had such a job to keep us all together: barking, puffing and blowing whilst we threw a stick for him to bring back. He was a fast runner and sprinter, he literally ran circles around us.

Hannie had a fun idea; we all would hide behind trees and let him find us.

Puffing with the effort of finding us, running off in different directions, he would howl and bark. Racing up and down from one to the other, whinging and whining if he missed, but howling with joy if he found us, and it sounded like he yodelled with such a crescendo when he found me, jumping up with glee.

No one had to walk him really. In those days there were no cars on the road and it was safe for him to air out around the block, but Frans liked to give him a long run on a leash with his bike, quite fast.

Freddy could run like the clappers and keep it up too, but even he would have to slow down after some stretch of road and meadows, it was amazing how he kept so fit on so little food.

No tins of dog food then, but it was a sort of thing between us, that we would all give him some food of our own, into his bowl. If we were not quick enough he would take it from our hands before we could get to his bowl. He was watching under the table to see who would reach down to him.

Of course my trick of feeding Freddy my red cabbage under the table, without being seen, did not always pay off. His customary sneeze gave the game away completely. Oh sugar!

Helmi Wolff

Mientje and our cat Trixy.

The Girl Who Saw Too Much

Dear Papa en Rien,   **August 1942**

Tonight it was thunder and lightning after the warm weather. I saw the lightning forking down and crashing with the thunderclap.

I got a bit scared and ducked under the table with Vicky

Mum took down the gleaming pot with the plant in it from the window seal, she said, "Don't be frightened, I think the angels are moving the furniture up there."

I got my own diary now from Hanny, she embroidered it with flowers and I write in it at night.

Are you alright Papa? We hope you can come back soon to us.

                Love from us all
                Mientje xxxx

Helmi Wolff

Lovely Freddy

Mum's remedy for recuperation and starting to feel good again, was keeping busy with useful work. She always did this herself, and expected the same from us.

New jobs were introduced, but for me it was one of a repeat, namely looking after Freddy even more, keeping him clean, with no fleas, groomed and happy.

Walking him often, he was my constant little companion, a faithful lively little friend, and I loved taking him on long walks; he never needed a lead, as he was obedient and smart.

One day coming back from the woods with him, I crossed the road leading home, when suddenly, dreaded Trieny appeared; she called out, "Mientje, your socks are sagging," and as I looked down to see, she sprang at me, with her two other brave friends, meaning to scare and bully me.

But she had greatly miscalculated.

Freddy growled and snarled like a lion, he sprang at her, baring his sharp teeth, ready to bite if she moved at all.

All three girls yelled and screamed as they ran off, Freddy in hot pursuit, until I called him back. I could just hear them shout, "Wait till I tell 'em, you'll get it."

It was amazing how brave that dog was. "Oh what a good little boy you are," I crooned. I was so proud of him, and did he know it too!

Arriving home he immediately stood over his food bowl.

Well how could I not spoil him a bit, my little hero!

The Girl Who Saw Too Much

Helmi Wolff

Apples under the Bed

Everything seemed as it was in my little bedroom. I loved to see my seven dolls sitting up in the old cot by the window, some smiled, but others looked sad, and one looked quite disturbed, well she had a bit of her foot missing and her face was scratched.

Sitting on the bed I remembered that I had stored some apples and pears under my bed, left over from the long summer. I had wrapped each one in some paper so that they would not touch one another and rot, like I had seen Mum do with the store for the winter. I could smell the apples, and I was hungry, well I could try one now.

Bending down to reach out I could see that the tray had been moved further back to the wall. I pulled it forward and saw immediately that it had been disturbed. I knew that I had nine apples left, but it did not look right. Unwrapping one I saw to my horror that a bite had been taken out of that one. I tried another and found the same thing there: four of them had been bitten.

I wanted to know who had done this, but I got a complete negative from asking both Frans and Hanny. How upsetting, no one owned up, it stayed a mystery. When I told Mum, she said, "We better make a nice apple mush of those then, before they turn."

"What lovely apple pudding this is," said Han, as she winked at Frans.

"Oh yes lovely," said he, as he turned reddish. I had not forgotten, and any time I heard some shuffling coming from my bedroom I rushed upstairs to see, but I never saw any one eating my apples, it must have been the wind.

There came a day that I was ill, some weeks later.

Having the measles was no fun, I had to be in the dark for ten days in case I'd get a blind eye, I was told. How horrible. It was quite frightening, fancy not being able to see Freddy or Mum or even Frans and Hanny, or any lovely blossoms.

I kept in the dark, and anyway my eyes were mostly closed with the accompanying high fever. Oh no! It was horrible being ill. Even while recovering it was difficult to read or do a drawing in the dark.

Mum kept sponging my forehead to cool me down which was so soothing, but I couldn't eat anything, and I got rather weak.

"When will this be over, Mum?"

"Soon," she said.

Eventually recovery came, but I was so listless, and in the dark. Mum brought a small pancake and that is when I discovered the little mouse that kept me company later during another illness, or was it the same one? The little squeaky voice came often, as if to say, "What have you got for me?" whilst balancing on his back legs, as cute as a button.

A light went up for me, regarding the apples under my bed – ahhh so now I knew who had taken many bites out of my precious apples.

Helmi Wolff

Lieve Papa en Rien Oct.1943

I am 8 years old now, for my birthday Vicky and I were allowed to have a small picnic in Orange Park, we looked at the aviary with the birds in it they are so lovely and one kept flying to me I gave it some of my bread, only a little as we only had one slice each. Vicky gave me a new ribbon in blue for my birthday, Mummy decorated my chair with crepe roses I sat on it for my favourite meal of bread pap, I wished you could have seen it, Papa.

Do you have a lorry, papa? Well I have to do my homework now Frans has done his and he has gone out with his new kite, it is so colourful, kiss, and kiss, Mientje.

Bad News

She just stood there, the letter in her hand, which was shaking, and she had turned a pale shade of grey.

Alarmed, Mientje tugged her arm and asked, "What, Mum, what?"

The postman said, "A letter from your Dad, Mien."

"Oh lovely," I muttered, knowing that Mum would be thrilled to see it, until she opened it and started shaking.

"Bad news," she uttered.

She forced herself to recover enough to re-assure me that Dad and Rien were alright, but I could see the change that had suddenly taken her by surprise. I wasn't quite sure what to think or do and all the time I was urging her to sit down and tell me. She looked at me sadly and said, "I have to go away for a few days Mien; Frans will look after you and give you dinner, I will leave a pan full of bean mash on the range, so you won't be lonely he?"

"Where are you going, Mum?"

"Rotterdam," came the reply.

The letter from Dad said that Rein had been taken to a 'concentration camp' as the Guards thought he was a Jew, since he was circumcised when he was little, owing to an infection, which was spotted, and a brutal arrest landed him in a notorious camp. The only way to prove that he was not Jewish would be with his Dutch birth certificate from Rotterdam.

Mother had to leave at once, she took the train and found that most of the inner city had been bombed and reduced to rubble, but Mum knew the minister, and that good man had managed to save the great seal and stamp of the church and town hall. He was eager to help and signed the birth certificate, with the great seal as proof.

This all took a while, but after two days I was so pleased to see Mum home when I got back from school.

"Lieve, Mien, would you like an appel flensje?" (Apple pancake). Oh wonderful!

There was so much to tell her about school and friends and not such friends. Then she looked at me and said, "We are all going on a little holiday, Mien, would you like that?"

How exciting is that? Frans loaded up the little cart with stuff for the happy holiday.

It was arranged for us to travel with our old next door neighbour in his lorry. It was the same one who had employed Rien in the past, as a carpenter.

It was about half a day's journey to a strip of land bordering No Man's Land, between Holland and Germany, near the town of Kleef, where a meeting with Dad's friend was to take place.

I was asleep again when we arrived. It was still early and the sun was just gathering strength, it all looked lovely to me, with trees and dry heather to run around in for play.

Frans produced two old blankets and a bedspread; he also found four long, straight sticks, which he stuck into the sandy ground, securing them with bits of stones.

The next thing was the string, which he knotted from corner to corner, while I wondered why we needed a washing line, but after the old blankets were secured on the top and the bed spread hung around the sides, all secured with clothes pegs, to make a sort of shelter. I squealed, "Oh a hut on the heather! Can I go in now, Frans?"

"Well, wait a minute; you can help me make a bed in there." Soft bed stuff was spread to lay or sit on; I knew I could sleep in there forever.

The Girl Who Saw Too Much

I knew nothing of the arranged meeting, but Mum and Frans looked out for a man in a lorry, who was employed to keep that strip clear of people who may cross there. Dad had described the man and his lorry in his letter, which miraculously got through scrutiny to reach Mother. It was actually quite dangerous to be there, although (I believe) we were just inside our border.

For three days we all waited, while I gathered flowers and looked at ladybirds etc, and then…! The expected lorry was heard nearing us and when it came in sight Mum and Frans started waving their arms wildly to attract attention. I thought it was a new game, so I joined them until it stopped.

Mum talked with the man, who was to take Rien's precious birth certificate to Dad. Mother got it from under her blouse, the one and only bit of paper to save her son's life, no photocopiers or duplicating machines then.

It was many years later, that I realised the agonizing uncertainty of the safety of this one piece of paper. All I saw at that time was that the man gave Frans some bread, water, meat and more in a big parcel.

That over, the little cart was packed neatly so it all fitted smugly again. Our old neighbour who had brought us appeared and helped to load it back in his lorry, and we were on our way back home.

Two weeks later a letter arrived from Dad to tell us that he got the certificate and, what is more, Rien was duly released from that atrocious camp.

"Oh thank God," Mum said with a trembling voice, tears of penned up anguish and emotion flowing over her face. She sank down on her knees and cried with happiness.

Our joy knew no bounds to know they were safe and well, and our customary home band was in full swing again, when the neighbours came to join us and Mum managed to make that funny tea stuff again for everyone. We looked like a delirious band of silly drummers with the cutlery hammering on the old oak table.

It was pure relief to know that the utterly dangerous situation, in which Rien had been thrown, was over.

In the evening we all wrote a letter to Dad and Rien and I drew a picture of our little hut camp on the heather.

The effects of this terrible experience stayed with Rien all his life, and after the effects of the brutal body torture were a living momentum. Much later, we saw how his three nails had been pulled off his fingers and his hair, which had also been pulled out in bunches to make him tell about other Jewish hide outs, never grew back, just tight, shiny skin patches. The scars of infected cigarette burn wounds, also due to the filth in which they were made to work and the lice ridden camp blankets were all over his body. But mostly his nervous system was irreparably affected, causing nightmares about having to march and stand on parade every morning to salute and shout 'Heil Hitler', whilst some of the prisoners were shot, or worse, in front of them. However, he invented an alternative, and shouted 'Drei Liter' instead. Marvellous! He was unable to tell us about all this, he tried once, but was overcome with the memory.

Many years later, when we both had our families, he did try to tell me a few atrocities, which are too painful and degrading to repeat.

The amazing rescue once my father had his birth certificate is as follows:

Dad went to the concentration camp, knowing that if his son was thought to be Jewish, he would certainly be so, but the birth certificate was conclusive. He was let in.

Dad asked for the commandant, who appeared quite soon, so Dad told him that a mistake was made in that they held a pure Dutch man for many generations. The certificate was absolute proof, Rien was brought in, and Dad was shocked at the sight of him, but they were then escorted off the premises.

Such relief is indescribable, but suffice to say, they escaped the dragon's teeth.

Rien also realised that in his employ at the carpentry-sawing mill there, he had actually helped to make the shelters for that camp.

Helmi Wolff

Blueberry Picking in the Woods

"Are you coming then Mien?"

"Yes, berry picking yes!"

Frans rode a long way into the woods over lots of tree trunks and stony roads, I never felt the crossbar of his bike so hard, up and down hills, flying along fast, round corners and cambering roads. I held on for all I was worth, whilst he seemed to be sailing and flying further and further in to the leafy lanes through woods and lovely shaded places.

It was exciting and I kept holding my breath with the concentration of staying on the bike, and not swaying too much, as that seemed really dangerous.

He was whistling a tune I knew, so I joined in, only to hear him say, "No don't do that, sit still and be quiet, I am whistling to make the birds sing. Yah?"

At last he stopped, "Right, here we are, get off now, Mien," he said.

Try as I may, I could not feel my legs, as for getting off, I would definitely need those.

"Come on," he urged, "this is a good spot, look it is blue with them, and there are the fox berries as well, they are worth more even."

Oh, I tried to move, but ***clonk***, fell promptly on my nose. Luckily the ground was soft with leaves and mud, and no way was I going to cry, but standing up was impossible. My legs just crumpled under me, as if they didn't belong to me at all. Eventually, tingling profusely, life came back to my poor little pins.

The Girl Who Saw Too Much

Serious picking started straight away. "Here, Mien," Frans said handing me an old enamel mug, "you pick this full, and then we will have that snack that Mum gave us."

Oh goody I thought, yes, *but* easier said than done.

It was a lot of bending and the berries tasted so good, I kept eating them. Of course I didn't know then how desperately my little body needed the vitamin C, I only wanted to gorge the sweet blueberries, but was still putting at least some of them into my mug.

My back ached so much almost straight away. I found if I sat down on my haunches, I could see them better and pick more, but then the bushes would tickle my legs and bum and the insects would crawl up into my pants.

"How are you doing, Mien, nearly full?" he asked.

"Um," but he could see the blue stains, not only on my fingers, but also around my mouth, what a giveaway. Well I could see that he had the same indelible blue dye all over his mouth too.

"Ah you are eating them; well try to fill the mug now."

Frans had picked four mugs full already, the basket's bottom was covered. He had to have at least two baskets full every time, to sell to the green grocer, and a little bit extra for Mum to make jam and stewed fruit or even some sort of dough berry bread. He had to earn a whole *'rijksdaalder'*, that is two and a half guilder, to pay for his bicycle licence again, which came in the form of a small brass plaque with a date stamp on it and four small holes through which a wire was threaded to wind it around the bike frame.

"When are we eating, Frans?" But he had rules:

"No I said a mug full, Mien get on with it now."

"Oh," at last I did start to pick in earnest, but they were a bit mangy, too wet really.

It started to cloud over and Frans got out the picnic. Mum even had included a drink, a bottle full of water and beet syrup, **oh lovely!**

I was nibbling away hungrily at my slice of bread, when suddenly, ***"Shh,"*** he whispered, "don't move, be still and look." A

great stag with at least twelve deer were looking at us only about fifteen metres away, and we were looking back silently for a long time perhaps a minute, then one of us probably moved a finger. The stag turned, and with him, the whole herd followed, galloping away deep into the woods. I was so impressed and excited about this sudden wonder that I could hardly concentrate on picking again.

"No not there," Frans said. I have already picked that clean.

"But, Frans, look there are lots left."

"Yes I know, they are too small, they will be ripe next week. Oh, and try not to squash them with your fingers." I always tried to keep close to him to feel safe, but he said, "No over there, Mien, go there."

We had been to these woods many times before, but it was always new to me again, because of the different things that grew there, mostly berries and tall pine trees.

One day sitting on a tree stump having our food he told me a story, from long ago. I was still in my pram apparently, and Mum, Hanny and he had pushed me in turn into the woods for a picnic.

They all started to pick blueberries, when suddenly a herd of wild swine thundered through the woods towards us all. There was no time to get the pram or to stand behind trees. "They travel in a straight line," Hanny shouted. "They won't bother us."

But one young swine strayed behind and looked into the pram, where I laid, (merrily chuckling away), to see if it was a mouse or a squirrel or such like.

But under loud shouting and shrieking from the lot of them he turned and ran off.

"Oh!" I said. "Would he have eaten me?"

"No," said Frans. "I think he took one look at you, and shrivelled up his nose in disgust."

Another time he told me that the sandwich Mum had made for us, is called after an English officer. Well I just giggled, surely no one could be called a sandwich, could they?

A picnic in the woods was exciting, it made every bit of bread taste extra special, and the fact that we were near starving probably had something to do with that.

Well the wind had got up a bit and at last it was time to go home.

"I tell you what, Mien, on our way back, we will go to the Juliana Tower." Oh that would be a treat, the Juliana Tower was a play garden, I suppose like an early Disneyland. It had a tall tower, of which you can glide helter-skelter, and some swings, also a seesaw and you could even buy lemonade there.

To get there, it was an even more hair-raising journey, and I had to hold the two full baskets of berries as well, but we got there a lot quicker than I thought. My feet felt like two sponges again, and I didn't trust myself to jump off with my heavy and fragile load. "I'll take that," said Frans. All right then, I managed to clamber down and followed him to the brightly painted gates.

The tower stood tall in front of us, it looked so big and I got a bit afraid. "Now," Frans said. "We go up the stairs on the outside, and then we sit on a mat, you go in the front and I will hold on to you." That was tempting; I'd love that of course.

It was scary to climb so high, but once at the top, I was almost giddy with looking at the view. "Now," he said again. "You sit on this coconut mat and I will be behind you." **Ouch** it was prickly but no time to think. He sat behind me and held me fast between his knees.

"All right then, here we go." We started to slide and all of a sudden we were swirling round and round the tower and then with a bump and a thud we hit the ground. The man took the mat and asked, "Want to go another time, son?"

"No more money," Frans said.

I was quite glad in a way as I started to feel queasy, but that wore off quite quickly, and I would have liked to try again.

The swings were next. Frans pushed me, it was such fun, and on the seesaw he sat one end and I on the other. Of course when he let go, I shot up into the air, whoosh!

There was some lemonade left and Frans spread his coat for us to sit on, I was almost too tired to drink any and we had a long way to get home still.

A short summing up and explanation here:

This part of Holland is called the 'Veluwe'. It has low hills and rolling countryside mainly with yellow sand, a lot of heather, some pine and little birch trees. It later reminded me of the 'New Forest' in England.

'The Juliana tower' was originally a lookout tower but had of later years been converted into a fun and play tower, like a helter-skelter, along with a few very simple other play things to make a children's play area. I believe now it has been made much more sophisticated.

Helmi Wolff

Lieve Papa en Rien   Nov 1942

I have drawn some stars in the sky. Do you see the stars at night, Papa? I learned that this big one is called Star of David, all the Jewish people have to wear a yellow band with that star on it round their arm, and even in their shops they have to have it on the window, now not many people go there as they have hardly anything left to sell. love and kisses. Mientje

The Girl Who Saw Too Much

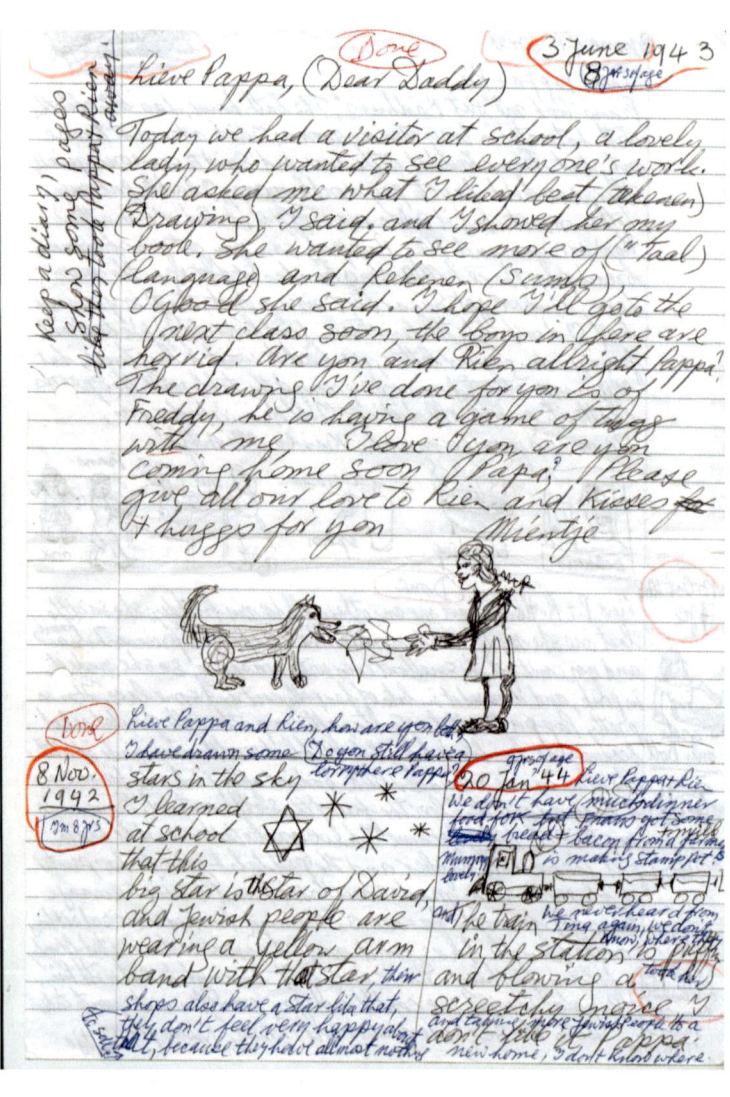

Helmi Wolff

Lemele Berg

Because of the food shortage, Frans had been told to look for accommodation for me at a kindly farm, to strengthen me up in my growing years, and to get me out of the firing line of the expected bombing of the bridges. One very amiable young but childless couple said yes they would have me for a few weeks to start with, to see if it worked out for them and for me! The first time in the summer time and thereafter perhaps also in the school holiday times.

The great day arrived, and I was all sixes and sevens, so I thought I'd take a last look at piggy in the shed, snuffling my hand when I gave him some grass, I patted him on his snout and said:

"They will look after you while I'm gone and you will grow too big for this shed, piggy."

Mum came in and she gave me a cuddle and a caution, more an instruction to be ever so good and take care not to break anything there, but also to tell me to write a little every day to her and to post it once a week.

"I've put your drawing and writing pad in the suitcase and Frans will give the farmer some money to post it."

The little suitcase was strapped onto the crossbar where he had welded my tricycle's saddle for me to sit on, another box sat on the back carrier, but the little cart he had made, with the back wheels of my tricycle, stayed behind this time.

"I've got enough peddling to do with you," he said.

The Girl Who Saw Too Much

We started early in the morning. Sixty kilometres was an enormous distance to cover, and Frans peddled on, but we stopped three times on route, to stretch my legs and eat a little of the picnic Mum had given us to take. I know that I fell asleep once because I felt myself tied onto him with two leather belts.

"What's this? I think I have to come down now," said I, with a still very sleepy voice.

"No not yet!"

"Where are we now?" Ah yes, I did have to be excused behind the nearest bush somewhere.

We finally arrived at our destination; the address read Lemele D 70. A little longhouse farm building surrounded by other similar ones all in a circle around the communal well and drain.

The farmer lady (quite young) came out of the house and stood by the front doorstep while we got of our bike. She rushed forward with open arms towards us, and in a very warm and welcoming voice said, "Oh, my dears you must be hungry after such a long journey," after which she ushered us indoors, and there on the table was a spread of delicious food, she had prepared for us.

What a feast it was. When we smelled the hot thick pea soup with lovely bits of lean bacon in it, it became very hard to keep our manners, particularly when she took us away to the deele, (the back house, where at night the animals sleep), to wash our hands and face in a bowl of water. She gave us a small towel to dry with and said, "Now we eat."

We were gorging ourselves when Mr Beimer (her husband) arrived at the back. When he spotted us, he said, "How do?" and sat down at the table with us. He was such a big man that I instinctively shoved my chair up a little to make space, he took a long look at me and said, "So you are Mientje, are you?"

A shy, "Yes, Mr Sir," from me. "And this is your brother, Frans, huh?"

"Yes, sir," Frans said.

"Well done, boy, that's a long way to peddle."

The friendliness of the pair soon put us at ease, and what with the warm glow of the fire my eyelids felt so heavy and I soon fell asleep almost at the table, but just before, I felt some big hands scoop me up and take me to what looked like a cupboard in the wall. Mrs Beimer opened the little doors and there was a lovely little bed freshly made.

I woke just enough to ask to go to the toilet first, which was out in the deele; I tried to climb onto the tall wooden plank with a large hole, which was a bit scary. I did not want to fall in to the bucket underneath, after that the little cupboard bed felt so comfortable.

When I woke up in the morning Frans had already left, but he put my little suitcase near the bed in the wall. Feeling refreshed from the long sleep, Mrs B. said, "Breakfast is ready, but first a wash, eh?" She had already fetched two buckets of water from the pump-well and poured some into the bowl we used yesterday.

"That's your bowl every morning and evening, Mientje," she said.

"Yes, Mrs B," I replied, at which she asked:

"Would you like to call me Aunty?" Oh I would, "Well then, you can say Tante en Oome' (Aunty and Uncle) to us."

Breakfast was a big boiled egg and proper bread, two slices, and a cup of milk. Oh boy I thought, this was real food, and I think it is going to be great. At the next-door neighbours I was introduced to their son, Henkie, he was about the same age as me but bigger and stronger. He looked at me quite nicely and asked, "Do you want to help me get the goat up the hill?"

Now that sounded like an adventure.

Little did I know that goats buck and bump, and that they wouldn't agree with anything you want them to do. This goat was called Hettie, and she was in a rather disagreeable mood, as she had not been milked yet. So here I got a lesson on how, sitting on a low three-pronged stool, very close to Hettie. After being shown what to do I soon got the hang of it, and later became quite good at comforting Hettie so I could milk her, it had a calming effect on me too.

"Come on, Mientje, we are done now, so we'll put the pan with the milk in the kitchen."

He put a collar and lead on Hettie (just like our dog I thought). We proceeded to lead her out of the deele and into the meadow, but once outside she started to buck and jump in an alarming fashion. I thought she'd choke herself doing that.

"Oei, oei, oei," goaded Henkie, getting her to go through the gate was almost impossible until she spotted the lush meadow out yonder, at which she nearly knocked him over as she belted out of the gate this time.

"Well now," said Henkie with all the authority the difference in our size afforded him. "Well now, see, you have to know what yer doin' see, with them goats, she was only looking forward to munching her lunch, Mientje!"

Mr B. came by, and patted Henkie on the head by way of, well done boy, but Henkie wasn't having his hair ruffled like that, like a kid, in front of the new girl. Smoothing his hair down again he asked, "Like to go up the mountain, Mientje?"

"Mountain?" I asked.

"Yes up there, I'll help yer." Of course that was Lemele berg itself, (Lemele hill). He must be thinking that I'm too weak; well I'll show him. I took a run and started to climb in a very stout fashion, but after a while it did seem steeper than I'd anticipated. So I invented a diversion, like: "Oh, Henkie, look at this flower." He looked at me with an expression like, 'Tired eh? I thought so!'

He had a great idea; he cut a long twig of a hazel tree and started whittling it a bit at one end with his pocket knife. I thought he was going to cut his fingers, but he expertly cut two groves at either end of the twig, and produced a bit of string from his pocket in his flannelette long shorts. He tied it strongly to one end and then carefully bent the twig as much as it would, to tie the string to the other end, and voila he had made a bow. That finished, he went in search of an elder tree, to cut half a dozen very straight sticks. I looked on intrigued but he soon got me working on those sticks too.

"Now look, Mientje, I'll cut 'em off straight at the ends, and you poke some of the soft stuff from the inside out see?"

"Oh yes I can do that." Poking my fingers in the ends it was quite soft and easily removed.

Henkie was cutting one half inch pieces of the discarded twigs, to fit over the other ends that had now become smaller in circumference to add weight to that end of our improvised arrows.

How clever I thought, and much later when I saw Frans again, I told him about it, but he said, "Oh I knew that already."

'Know all,' I thought, but he'd take me on a sharp shooting expedition one day, he promised.

Anyway Henkie and I were ready; I'd seen some rabbits there. "Now I'll show 'ee," said Henkie. He strutted the bow aside his shoulder, stretched the string, whilst holding the arrow alongside it and aligned it with much ado. Suddenly, PAFF, he let it go, it fell about five metres away from us.

"You 'ave a go, Mientje." He gave me the bow and showed me how to hold and straighten the arrow in my sight. He found a stone and said, "Shoot that, right, aim," he shouted. "Pull," he said. "Let go," he bellowed. PHUFF, it landed just about one metre in front of me.

I ran to see and shouted accusingly, "That's because this arrow was crooked, see there is a notch in it."

"Not bad for a beginner," Henkie mumbled. He gave me a new arrow. I inspected it and could find no fault. Ah I will pull the string tighter this time and shoot it further, ahha, and it flew all of three metres.

"Now," Henkie said. "You are ready for a moving target." Oh that was progress indeed. We laid down low in the long grass and waited for a rabbit to show up, I knew that it could not really hurt too much with these blunt soft arrows, but we sorted out the best one.

After a while we saw some movement and Henkie trained his arrow on that. PAFF, it flew, and just as it hit the ground we saw the rabbit jump out and away from us. "Ah well," said Henkie, "You have a go now, Mientje." I had really got into the game and determined to do better. I stretched the bow so far that, to my horror, it snapped in two.

"Oh sorry," I said.

"Never mind," replied Henkie. "I'll make a better un next time."

I liked Henkie, but I did not always want to go out playing with him, even though he called every day for me. Sometimes I just wanted to stay home and do some drawing and writing etc., or help Aunty B. One day she said, "I think you are getting fat here, Mientje, with all the good food." Was I?

"You can help me make sand patterns in the front room." They had a front room? I thought that I'd seen it all, when she opened a door behind a curtain which I had not spotted before. There **was** another room with sand on the floor. Narrow wooden benches were arranged flat against the wall and in the middle hanging low from the ceiling was a beautiful oil lamp made of coloured glass and brass fittings. "Can you help me sweep the sand nicely, and then we'll make patterns in it, to look like a new design."

We had to sweep it in round swirls and pick up anything like rubbish, and after that she showed me how to finish it by hand in pretty patterns, like shells and flowers. She was pleased with my few additions and I thought I'd draw my little dog Freddy in the sand, but that was not acceptable and had to be erased. She asked me if I missed my dog. I nodded, but told her that I liked Hettie the goat. But I actually wanted a hug from my mum, and see all my friends, even if I was making friends here and meeting very kind people.

Mr B came in and asked, "Can you help Henkie catch a chicken today, Mientje?" I accepted enthusiastically, that would be a great game. It never occurred to me the reason for catching one would be to eat it! The chickens were loose in a field and Henkie and I ran and ran after them trying to grab one, but every time we almost did, the chickens ran away flapping and cackling for all they were worth. We tried again after lunch without even touching one. Mr B. came by again, and said, "How many now?"

"Not even one, Uncle," I said. Henkie quickly put on his cap in case he ruffled his hair again. But the great man just put down his hand; the chickens strolled by quietly clucking away, and one of them simply strolled under his hand, quick as a flash he had caught it.

Henkie and I just looked on amazed; our mouths must have dropped to our chins. "How did he do that?" I said. "You know, Henkie, that one you almost caught, well he had special running legs, long as a pair of under trousers."

Henkie laughed out loud and said, "Silly, how'd you think that chicken could run with trousers on?"

"Well," I said, "we had a chicken once and he ran away and my Dad ran after it, but he couldn't catch it, and my Dad can do anything."

"So can mine," said Henkie, "but we have cows and you don't have to catch those."

That evening, we had the most delicious meal. The meat was light, and so tender. I tucked in, and after a while the conversation between my new aunt and uncle veered round to the day's events. "You should have seen those little uns look when I caught this un, they'd been trying for hours to catch one, and by gum it's a tasty un, isn't it, Mientje?"

I stopped in my tracks when suddenly I realized that we were eating that lovely chicken, and that it was not a game after all. The bit that was in my mouth would not go down; it completely stuck in my throat.

"You can help digging up some tatties de morrow," he said.

That night in my little cupboard bed I dreamed that the other chickens chased us and that we could not get away. In my sleep I wet the bed, and to make matters worse I was wearing the panties that mum had died black for school. Of course the dye came out and stained the sheets. I was so embarrassed trying to dry it off with my towel which then also got soiled. Running to the deele where the toilet bucket was, I lost my footing, made a clatter falling on some milk pans, which started the one and only cow mooing, which in turn woke Aunt and Uncle.

They were quite upset and in the morning, I had to help wash the sheets and stretch them on their bit of lawn out the front. I was so embarrassed that I wished for the ground to swallow me. When Henkie came round, I was really hoping that he would never know, I'd never live it down.

Mr B. said we could dig the potatoes now, and he gave us some steal tops which we had to put on our fingers. Mine kept coming off and I kept losing them in the soil, so it took me a lot longer to fill a basket with the lovely white and other red potatoes. Henkie was loosening the earth around the plants with a fork. I had never seen potatoes come out of the earth; Mum always bought hers from the greengrocer's cart that came round our street once a week.

Saturday night arrived and I could see it was very special to them as they were both wearing their best clothes. It was their turn to entertain the neighbours in their front room. The curtain was swept back and the secret door opened, revealing the new floor patterns I'd helped with.

I was told that it was my bedtime now, so to get washed and ready. While I was using the wooden toilet I could hear lots of different voices. These were the people arriving for the evening's entertainment.

Dare I peek to see who these were? Better not after the last embarrassing episode of the wet bed. I could hear a man's voice starting to sing. He was telling a story in verse, a loud applause followed and for the first time I heard Aunt B. sing. She had a nice voice but she was wavering a lot with her tuning. Oh I thought they want to have Mum playing the piano for them.

I was dying to have a peek, but I tried to constrain myself. However, when I heard Uncle B. sing a 'hopsa daisy song' (as Dad would have called that) I slipped out of bed and unseen by anyone peeked from behind the curtain, which was halfway over the secret door.

Who were all these chattering people? I saw two of them kissing, just under that lovely low oil lamp on the floor! Quickly I slid back into bed before anyone noticed me. I fell asleep with all the singing and laughter in my ears.

The next morning after a good wash with fresh water from the well pump, Aunt B. gave me a lovely cup of hot chocolate and told me that Frans would be fetching me to go back home tomorrow. It surprised me, and Aunt B. gave me such a tight hug, as if she did not want me to go yet. I looked at her and a few tears were being wiped away. I felt loved by her and in a strange way I also loved her as an aunty, but I had missed my mum and even Frans and Hanny and all the rest.

We had to get up in good time for Frans to get to us by breakfast time. Whatever time must he have started from home? I thought. It really was good to see him again. He said, "Mien, you have grown,"

"Yes," I said. "It is all this good food. And Henkie and I keep running and getting stronger."

On the way home I was almost too big for my little saddle, but he did tell me that he had to pay a little extra for two new sheets. Oh he knew about that! I was so ashamed. Luckily he had some money left for a few stops along the way home, at a real restaurant where I drank lemonade.

Many years later when I was in Holland again, I visited, 'Arnhem open air museum'. I was amazed to see this very village completely transported from Lemele to the museum, with the well in the middle and some of the older grass plaque houses with the roofs touching the floor. There in the middle of the circle was the little long house with the room, which contained my little cupboard bed.

Helmi Wolff

It had all been brought there and resurrected as if it was all still in use. The number on the door of that little farm from the past was D70. I took photos and wondered what had happened to the people who had lived there.

The Girl Who Saw Too Much

Liesje's Party

Liesje van Hoeven, a rather shy but quite sly girl, asked me if I would like to come to her birthday party. I was amazed since she was actually one of them, who had joined in the tickling horror, and had actually been the main one to tie me up with her skipping rope. I had been staying well clear of her ever since.

I was thrilled to be asked, and a little too eager in my acceptance, thanking her very much – a bit over the top. Her smile faded somewhat, in the face of my transparent joy. Puzzled I wondered why but it became quite clear later, when she said, "And wear something new and pretty," looking at my adapted altered dress and worn left boot with a smirk.

Hardly anyone had a real party, and I was not quite sure about what was required for it.

A present for her, maybe a new dress? The moment I got home, I burst through the door with, "Mum, guess what, I have been invited to Liesje's birthday party."

"Well **wow**," she said. "You see, you do have friends?"

"Well yes, but what shall I wear, Mum?" Now that really was a loaded question, **what indeed?** The little black and white chequered dress that Liesie's mum gave me was much too short now. I had shot up a bit since then, and my thin legs looked waif like showing under the short skirt, but the waist was still the right size.

It had mostly been worn for Sunday best at church and Sunday school. Hardly anyone in my school had seen it before. Mum found a long black skirt that had been left behind by one of my older sisters.

"Yes," said Mum, "that could come in very handy," She cut a wide strip off the bottom and started to sew it onto the little dress like a pretty flounced rouse. It did not take long and after a short while, she said, "Try it on now, Mien." It sure covered my bony knees and it fitted; she held up a mirror, yes it looked pretty.

"Oh, lovely, Mum, thank you." I was overwhelmed with relief, it looked new and lovely. Next, two cast iron smoothing irons were heated on the glowing hot range, after a bit of pressing and stroking out of the creases of the new flounce, my party dress was ready to be tried on again. As I admired myself in the mirror, twirling round I saw that Mum had brought in her black hat with a long ribbon.

I was just going to protest at wearing a hat. I did not want to wear one but then I saw her undo the long ribbon. She draped it round my waist, and tied it into a small bow at the back like a sash.

I was lost for words but tears welled up in my eyes, and then I saw that Mum also pinked away a tear. "What a great cuddle you are," she said. Suddenly I realized that we could be creasing it again, so I quickly let go and said, "I feel so posh in this frock."

Mum helped me take it off, after which she did a bit more ironing on the skirt, but oh no, the irons had got too hot and a small hole was burned just to the right of the front. Horrified I watched.

"Don't worry," she said as she fetched the by now shortened, long black skirt again and cut out a heart shaped pocket, and sewed it over the burn hole on the dress. A white lacy handkerchief was found and displayed in the pocket to peep over the top, and after it was also sewn into place. She said, "You can wear it to school on the Tuesday, ready to go to the party straight after."

Mum wrapped another pretty embroidered hanky for a present in some of Frans's coloured kite parchment paper. "Now you have to make a card, Mien, you can use a bit of the left over paper," she said.

I did not want to make it soppy so I just wrote, from your class mate, Mien.

Helmi Wolff

I Had Hardly Been Able To Concentrate On My Lessons All Day

Teacher noticed, and kept asking me to read, or give answer in the geography lesson and when I nearly made a mistake in arithmetic, I thought, 'Oh no, I must not get detention tonight or I'll miss Liesje's party'. But the long awaited gong sounded and everyone stood sedately next to their desk, before the sign was given to allow us all to file neatly out of the classroom.

Liesje's mother collected us all from school. She was waiting at the gate. I had been concerned not to sit on my lovely dress all day and I managed to fold it so that the skirt had got pleats downwards.

Everyone was chattering, and Liesje's mother noticed that I was left rather on my own. I saw a one cent coin on the pavement, but I did not dare pick it up for fear of looking paltry or poor, but Gerda Buiter did pick it up and showed it to the others. I kept just behind the mother who looked at me very kindly and actually took my hand. I thought this might look like a bit of preferential treatment and could land me in trouble again, so I let loose and politely said, "It's all right, Mrs van Hoeven, I can keep up, thank you for inviting me."

"Oh!" she said, "it was Liesje who asked you to come."

Their house was a lot bigger than ours, and it seemed very grand to me. The lounge was enormous and decorated so richly with big leather chairs, a sofa and matching brown curtains. I could not help thinking that if our carpet was as light and as patterned as theirs, Mum would have hung it on a wall instead.

The Girl Who Saw Too Much

The long kitchen table was laden with food. Nice little sort of jelly things stood on plates all round the table for each of us. I could hardly wait to eat such a delicacy, but feigned slight indifference, as if I was used to such luxury. My eyes lit up when in the middle of the feast a marvellous cake was carried in with nine small candles burning on the top.

How many coupons would this take I wondered, but that is something you do not ask on such an occasion.

Cakes were something my mother was not big on; pancakes, yes, or fried sopped bread, but cake was the stuff you got when visiting aunties and uncles after church.

We all helped Liesje blow out her candles, and that is when I realized that I was a full one and a half year younger than her. I should have realized as I was so much smaller, but then I started school before six, and Liesje had to do her year again making her older than her peers.

Gerda had some jelly in her mouth and when she helped to blow the candles out, the jelly also flew out and landed across the table on Willie's plate next to me. She looked crossly at Gerda and signalled that she was a rotten shot. I was a bit puzzled at that but a wink of Gerda in my direction was enough to tell me that it was meant for me. I think I blushed deep red, but in the general euphoria of the happy birthday song for the birthday girl my embarrassment was not noticed, except perhaps by Liesje's mother.

Mrs van Hoeven cleared the plates. I made to help but she put her hand on my arm and said, "Just join in the games and enjoy yourself, Mientje."

Blind man's Buff was a starter. I was chosen by Liesje to be 'IT', and was duly blindfolded with a scarf over my eyes and nose, I could hardly breathe. Next I was spun round and round and round till I was very dizzy.

The command *'run'* was given and I stumbled a bit, but managed to keep upright, trying not to winch with the pain of my left foot, which had got slightly twisted in the fall.

Running was still not quite possible but eventually, I made the effort, only to find that my other foot was painful too. I kept stumbling and seeing stars with the searing pain and when the floor met me again, feeling utterly miserable, a strong soft hand pulled me up.

Liesje's mother took of the scarf and said, "I think you have hurt yourself, Mientje." The sudden light hit me and darts of pain went through me.

Seeing her, at least I knew that I had spoiled the game. "Oh no," I uttered.

"Don't worry," she said. "The game will go on, but I better have a look at your foot, eh?"

Shouting above the din she told them to continue carefully, and taking me into the lounge she sat me down into one of the huge chairs, I could feel my ankle swelling up and asked her not to take off my boot being embarrassed I pretended to be fine.

"Now, Mientje," she said, "I only want to look and make it better. I won't show it to anyone." I winched as she took off my knee stockings and looked at both my feet. Her hands were so cool and soothing while she softly massaged both feet.

To distract me she showed me the beautiful pictures on the walls of the room. I recuperated a bit and started to relax somewhat. There was a huge mantelpiece over the enamelled hearth; I was very impressed with the beauty and size of it all and with all the photographs in silver frames on top.

I tried to stand up but sank back into the leather chair, at that Liesje came in and asked if I was coming back to play, but before I could answer her mum said, "In a minute, dear."

She was looking at me and gesturing towards the photos, she asked if I would like to look at them closely. Oh yes I would love to, so while passing the biggest one of a beautiful bride and groom down to me she said, "That was me on my wedding day with my husband." She added that he had also been taken to Germany by the Gestapo. Just like my Dad and Rien, I thought. She said that he would not be coming back to her; astonished I asked **why**. "Well," she said, "he is not alive anymore."

At that my eyes filled up with tears thinking of my Daddy and brother so far away too. She started to hug me and wipe my tears. I was embarrassed again but she showed me another photo of Liesje's sister; she looked younger than Liesje about four or five years of age, I thought. She told me that she was called Greta, but she had diphtheria, and passed away; having no idea what that meant I thought that maybe diphtheria was a lovely flower, but did she sniff it too hard and what was passing away? Maybe somewhere nice?

She looked sad, and I did not have the heart to ask, so I thought to compliment her with, "They are lovely frames."

"Ah," she said dreamily. "Not even good enough for those."

She asked me if I wanted to rejoin the party but only sit in a chair for the next game. The light was dimmed again and Liesje's mum and aunty (who had been hovering in the background) were holding up a white sheet at each end tightly, but because it was dark you couldn't see anything.

One of the girls had a torch and was holding it up at the top of the sheet. We were told in a really sort of howling creepy voice that it was a ship on the stormy sea. We had to follow the light with our eyes very closely, while the torch wobbled from side to side, going ever deeper from the horizon and suddenly down to the bottom.

"Shipwreck," was the cry. A cold wet thing hit my face, with shouts of: "Shipwreck, hit the water we have hit the rocks, abandon ship."

Getting thoroughly soaked I screamed in panic, of course it was only a wet sponge.

I was helped to go out into the corridor hall, where all the other girls were lined up to wait for their go. I had certainly christened the game with my screams, but I refused to tell about what had happened, even when pressed to tell, and so I felt that I was regaining some of my dignity and composure amongst them.

After the party was over, Liesje's mother insisted on bandaging my ankle tightly in vinegar soaked strips of cotton, before carefully walking me home, and explaining to my mum why I had a sprained ankle.

There was no room in my head to talk about that anyway. "Well guess what," I spurted out, I had so much fun and games and, lovely food, and even Frans got jealous. I heard him utter a moan when he heard about the **jellies and cake**.

The Girl Who Saw Too Much

Wijna and Hanny with Mia and Fransie –
my beautiful niece and nephew.

Helmi Wolff

Kite Flying and a Photograph

Frans had been given some brightly coloured waxy parchment paper for his birthday, together with thin string and some bamboo sticks, which he split into four down lengthwise to be used as stays for his Kite in the making. The paper was beautiful, bright red, yellow and blue.

"Put your finger in the middle of the kite cross for me Mien, I'll tie it together."

I tried to hold still and press my finger down hard. "Oh that's useless, hold still," he barked. "Can't you press harder?"

"Ouch," I yelled. "Don't tie my finger in the knot Frans." He yanked the string upwards fast and my finger popped out again.

While I was sucking my painful finger, he attached the string from corner to corner. I could see now how it started to look like a kite shape. "Ah," I uttered, whilst he laid it onto the red paper, cutting out the shape most carefully, and leaving enough border to glue round the string.

I was hoping for some little off cuts, to use for our dolls house, but after helping to make the tail bows, I could see that took almost all the rest. We started to knot the tail bows into the string. "We have to leave it now for a while, to dry the glue," he said (which was a little starch Mum had donated for the purpose). "It will shrink a bit when the paper contracts," he said. *More gobbledegook,* I thought.

Later I saw what he meant. The kite lay there shining tight, and 'contracted', ha-ha, I thought, a brand new word for our saga play.

The next day it rained buckets so we couldn't get out, but the following day it was bright and lovely. I could hardly wait for Frans to come home from school, as he had promised me that I could help to fly the wonderful kite.

At last there he was. "Yes wait for a bit Mien, I need to go upstairs first." It all took far too long. Impatiently I called upstairs for him to come down. "Yes, yes, alright then, you still want to help me fly my kite?"

"Yes I do."

Out of breath, but almost getting to the field behind the 'Jagers weg', I remembered that Vicky was waiting for me to call round. "You will have to do that later otherwise I'll get someone else to help."

No competition at all then, I would have to go later. "Hold the kite loosely by the bamboo, like so, see? Loosely but steady I said!" shouted Frans as he ran backwards with the string, and then suddenly:

"Let go, Mien, **now**!" I let go and I could feel the pull of the string and wind. Slowly, carefully it ascended into the air and Frans pulled on the handle he had made to control the flight. I let the long tail drag over my open hand, to merrily fly behind the colourful kite.

Frans had stopped running backwards; he was caging the pull of the wind to let it fly and soar bit by bit until it flew high into the blue sky, and became only a small object very far away.

He kept pulling the string powerfully but gently as well, it was beautiful.

Soon other boys and girls came out to fly their kites, until there were so many in the sky, I was hoping that the strings would not get tangled. I thought it was the most gorgeous display, and very clever to keep the kites flying so high.

One day when I had almost got home from school, Henkie ran up to me, telling me that Frans had cut his head on a barbed wire fence running backwards and that lots of blood had run down his face. Mum had taken him down to emergency in the Juliana Hospital, at the end of our road. I ran home to find no one there. I ran to the hospital to see Mum and Frans just coming out.

Frans had a bandaged head; three stitches he told me, with a certain amount of bravado. Mum smiled and said, "He never cried, Mien!" Oh well he looked OK, and the white sort of bandage hat looked quite jaunty I thought.

That evening he had no homework from school, so he was free to pursue his hobby of photography He had made a pinhole large tin camera, and yesterday he had left it in the sun for a while pointing at a stationary object. I had seen it, but was told not to go that way in case it would fall, so I had been quite curious to know what on earth it meant.

I was not to enter his room either, but curiosity caused me to break that rule one day, and so when he was out I gingerly entered. Well I can't say I saw a lot as the window had been completely blacked out and every tiny gap in the woodwork of the sloping roof was filled in with bits of paper all painted black, what a disappointing discovery.

But this time Frans said, "Do you want to see something, Mien?"

"Oh yes I do please."

"Well in a moment you can come into my room, just wait till I call you." *An exciting mystery*, I thought.

"Come in then," he called. Oh his room had been altered. It was quite light, but there was a big wardrobe cupboard at the end near the bed, and it was painted black. Carefully he opened the doors. There was a little stool against the end. "Sit there, nice and still, Mien, and watch."

"Yes."

A longish plank was hammered against the long end of the wardrobe with sort of brackets to be a workbench. On it stood his strange tin pinhole camera and a tray with some liquid in it, also a torch, which had some of his orangey red parchment paper, tied round the glass.

He closed the double doors; it was pitch black in there until he switched on the torch after charging it with its ratchet, revving it up a few times very fast. He put a pair of pinchers on the ratchet to keep it working.

"What?" I started.

"Shush, just watch now," *right!* When he opened the tin camera, there was a piece of paper, which he laid into the tray with the liquid. "Watch," he said again.

Oh this is magic, there before my eyes was the image he had captured by pointing it at the shed window behind which he had put some paper flowers, left from our birthdays. I could not believe my eyes.

"What do you think, Mien?" he asked.

"Well it is marvellous, how did you do that?"

"Ah that is for another time. Don't open the doors till I tell you now. This is for my school," he said, "but I'll do it again with your dolls if you like? Then you can colour it in and make it into a card for a birthday!"

Helmi Wolff

Piggy Pots, Rabbits and Cold Work

I could hear the squealing indoors. "Better go and look," said Mum.

As I approached, the shed door was open. Wim was inside, and he was looking at his rabbits, feeling their back legs. I asked why he was squeezing them, as I had been feeding them all the grass and dandelions I could find all this time. "Never you mind, Mien, you ask too many questions," I was told, which seemed strange to me, as I had always thought, 'if you don't ask you will never know'.

"Anyway," I proffered. "Piggy pots is hungry, Wim, have you got anything to give him, Wim?" Waiting expectantly, Wim snorted, and that was all the reply I got for now, presently he asked me if I had seen my sister Wijna.

"Not today," I said.

"Well go to see her she has got somik for ye."

"Oh." Flying out of the shed I went to see, it was only a few doors up the road, and it was no time at all before I got to their back door. I could hear my tiny nephew, the youngest, called 'Frans' also, cooing, and my darling little niece Mia saying soft little singing words to him, Oh how sweet, I loved them so much; they were like a little sister and tiny brother to me.

Wijna called out from the front room, "Can you take them for a walk, Mien, as I have so much sewing to do." I could hear the hand sewing machine whirring furiously. Overjoyed to be asked, I called back, "Yes I will, when do you want me back, Wijna?"

It became a regular feature that I would call after school, to take the little ones out for a walk. In the good weather I was allowed to take them to the park and sit on a bench while we played with each other. Mia loved looking at the birds there and I liked to tell her stories about them, like how they talk to each other, with all the necessary bird noises and animal voices to accompany the tale. Even the flowers often took on voices of their own. I fantasized about their relation to each other and Mia was fascinated. She used to join in to my delight, and make little voices also.

When school holidays were on, Wijna gave me lots of other jobs to do and for that I could have some dinner with them. I was pleased to help with their young family; I loved the children.

It was Christmas holiday and I tried to do the washing in the freezing back annex, of the small, unheated cottage, it involved stamping and stomping the dirty clothes with long stompers, in two stone washbasins as hard as I could.

I was tiring a lot, and it was so cold, when Wim came through. "You will never make a washerwoman like that," he said. I tried a bit longer, but thought, 'I don't want to be a washerwoman anyway,' so I gave up, only to be asked to peel half a bucket of potatoes in the coldest water, in that icy annex.

"There are still 'pits' in them," he said, when I brought them into the kitchen all peeled, "see?" he insisted. "You have missed these, they are like eyes see? Do them again," he commanded. I was so cold and disgusted, that I threw down the knife which was almost cramped in my bony hands, before running out of there and down the road to Mum; but not before I stopped to gather the potato peelings in my apron for our hungry piggy pots with the tears streaming down my face.

"What ever happened, Mien?" she asked. Sobbing I told her. "Oh come on now, Mien, don't cry. You won't have to go there again this winter, even if we have to find another mouth to feed, we will pray and then we will manage, love."

After I stopped crying, and having warmed up by the range, I recovered a bit.

Mum had made some sopped bread and even if it was that nasty almost black stuff, it never tasted so good, and I remembered that I had some peel for piggy, who had heard me running by, ah.

The Girl Who Saw Too Much

Lieve Papa en Rien,   Feb 1943

Today we had a visitor at school, a nice lady, who wanted to see everyone's work. She asked me what I liked best. Drawing I said, I showed her my book, but she wanted to see more of writing and reading and sums. Oh good she said. I hope I'll go to the next class soon; the boys in here are horrid.

Are you and Rien alright, Papa? The drawing I have done for you is of Freddy dog and I.

We are having a tug of fun with his old rag. I miss you Daddy, can you come home soon? Love to you and Rien hugs and kisses.

                     Mienje

Helmi Wolff

The Sergeant's Bike

Money was almost completely useless, it had hardly any value. Our lovely Dutch coins had been replaced with German money specially minted for our overrun and occupied country – horrible lightweight lead coloured coins which were like a porous sort of metal and liable to snap in two in your pocket. Money alone would not buy anything if you had no coupons to go with it.

Coupons were always in short supply, thus everyone ran out of them long before the next date of issue. At the butchers' Mrs Jongeling tried hard to convince him that the date on her ticket was now; while she held her finger over the bit of scribbling that had given the game away of her trying to alter the date. "I am sorry Mrs," said the butcher, "but if everyone did that, there would be even less to go round."

"Yes but…" she started again almost crying now. "My husband is away and I can't make ends meet with eight kids."

The butcher was a kind man and he was sorry for everyone. He gave her some tripe that he had extra and some terrible looking offal. Mum said, "Don't cry, dear, I'll send you some potato cakes, with Mientje!" Oh, I could eat that myself I thought!

Frans had again been able to get some milk and grain, plus a lovely piece of fat from the farmers, and I was happy to bury two stone bottles full of creamy milk in the hole behind our house. "Come in afterwards now, Mien," Mum said. "I have kept a lovely beaker full here for you to drink straight away."

The little door of the secret cupboard was open. I had never seen this, as it was so well hidden in the alcove corner of the room with the same wallpaper stuck over it, so as not to show up at all. But I spotted the dreaded cod-liver oil bottle there tucked away on a small triangular shelf.

Oh no, that stuff tasted so awful and the smell alone would start me retching. Mum saw me look and pulled me on her lap. "Now," she said, "you must forget about that small cupboard and never even look that way; you know who would take it all, and it is the only food we have."

She looked so serious, that I knew it was very important to follow her instructions. And I did, to the letter.

"What is the matter with your neck," said Hanny, next time she saw me jerk my head away from that direction.

"Oh nothing," I replied.

"Stop shaking your hair then." I sort of smiled secretly, and thought, I knew something important.

Mum looked very pleased when she came home from a short visit to Mr Jouwstra. "Gather round all of you," she said, in a very sort of subdued but excited way. "We won't be at war much longer." Looking into our expectant faces she continued. "You must not tell anyone, or make a lot of noise about it, as the person who told me, could get into trouble." She never told us where she gleaned that information.

Much later I heard that old Mr Jouwstra up the road had a secret wireless set he had made himself with some valves and magnets, I think, with which he could receive news from the liberating army and also from the Germans.

He must have been eighty at the time. Luckily he never got found out, but the hope and real relief that came with that news was marvellous. Everyone seemed more able to cope and even cheerful to know that Nymegen had been freed, and that Arnhem must surely be next after which Apeldoorn could not be far behind.

I had heard of underground workers, but I simply thought that these were people who worked under the ground. Many, who like my mother helped to save lives if possible, in all sorts of complicated and secret ways. Some, who were caught, were not only never seen again but were made an example of, like the dreadful day when dead bodies were laid out on the corners of the road to frighten and scare us all. These were the men who had tried to ambush the car of the brutal Gestapo leader in our area. They are the unsung heroes to whom we are so grateful.

Of course I never knew how many brave people tried to help to alleviate and shorten the war but our old Doctor Foster was one such a man, who at a great age, swam across the canal to the liberation front, to give information as to where to cross, and how the workers on the other side could assist and guide. He had several goes at the crossing under cover of a very dark night while being shot at in the water but eventually got through. When a new doctor took over his practice we thought that he must have been killed, but we heard later that he had gone into hiding, and that he lived another ten years after the war.

Mum had to go out for a while again to see a friend, so I thought I'd go to see Mrs Dulland. I'll just pick some flowers on my way from the hedges and grass verges; she would like that. "Ah, Mien, just what I need," she said. "I have dropped the sponge, can you pick it up for me, and rinse it in the bucket there please? Yes that's it hand it up to me now." Mrs Dulland was up the ladder cleaning her windows. "I'll be down in a tick," she continued. Water dripping down my neck from the wet sponge I reached as high as I could. "Oh ta!" she said. "Come in, I'll see if I have got something to give you, Mien."

I told Frans that Mrs Dulland gave me a peppermint sweet for helping her. "That's funny," he said. "I have raked her bit of front garden once, when she was up a ladder, and all I got was a wet sponge thrown onto my neck. 'Yes,' I thought, 'she does like cleaning windows a lot!'

I often looked at Mum's glass bookcase, which was kept locked, as some of the books were not yet deemed suitable for my age. I wondered why, and how old would I have to be, before I would be allowed to read some? Instead of having to knit a stupid blue cotton towel for school, in handy crafts? I was told that it was good for my karma, well now what was that then? It was something to do with endless patience I realized later.

The waterworks in our roads had been damaged again; we could only get water from the tank, which came round at night. I was thirsty but I knew better than to drink from the saved water of the washing, so we all waited for the cart with the water tank. Mum knew what to do. She boiled some of the water on the range and made some sort of gruel pap and a cup of tea! Well how did that happen? It was made with the finely shredded bark of the pine tree and the resulting powder roasted in the oven, which ended up remarkably like the taste of tea, or had we all forgotten what that was supposed to taste like?

For me the prospect of our cosy cellar at night was not so bad, in fact it was quite a comfort to think about; especially if, sometimes Frans went to stay with his friend across the road where they had a bigger cellar. Then Mum and I had our own whole cellar to ourselves and we could sing all our favourite songs and ditties. But it was only afternoon and Mum had returned to give us some smothered bread, which she soaked in milk and if possible an egg mixed in and some sweet beet syrup for flavouring, after which she fried individual bits in the dripping bacon fat that was caught – it was so yummy.

Frans and I started to do our homework from school, when we noticed some commotion across the road at Mr Boomgaard's who had a monumental stonemason yard. Mr Boomgaard and his son

Helmi Wolff

Beekie could be heard hammering and chipping away at the marble and granite. Above it all, Beekie's strong singing voice rang out in notes bright and clear, in perfect timing with his hammer. He usually sang popular tunes of the moment, often patriotic reels of all sorts.

This time he had not only engaged in singing the Royal Anthem, but this had now been bent into a real belittling verse, meant to aggravate the oppressors, and then followed it by sniggering and shouting, "Up the Orange, down the Black," and more, really taking the mickey, calling them Jerries etc. Just as he was going to sing a similar ditty, a German soldier on his bike came riding by and had obviously heard the offensive song.

Oh well, he got of his bike with some difficulty as he was quite fat, and with great importance parked his beautiful machine at the gate. Sticking out his chest, he marched into Mr Boomgaard's yard shouting, ***"Schwine hund,"*** and more.

Startled, Mr Boomgaard and Beekie looked up, and walking towards him, cap in hand both of them, asked, "Do you need a gravestone sir?"

Beekie got nervous. He knew that he had offended him with his singing, and turning his cap round and round in his hand, he started to apologize, but his dad repeated his question: "Do you need a gravestone, sir?" A bit more urgently, at which the soldier noticed that Beekie was slightly retarded. He started poking him about saying, "Sing for me, sing for me, go on!"

But Beekie only laughed shyly, rolling his cap around and looking at his battered boots, at which, the soldier started to roar, like a laughing hyena. It was then that the father asked, "Have you got a leak? Has your tyre gone flat?" At that the soldier looked round, and to his consternation, his bike had gone. Oh dear, he ran to see, but his bike was nowhere to be seen. He ran to look round corners of the road. It was magic, and, these 'verukte Hollanders' had something to do with that. Well yes!

Apparently two boys from the next road had pinched the formidable machine, with air tyres and all. They had been watching him park, and as soon as the soldier was out of their sight, had silently taken it, running fast through an aunt's garden and a hedge, over a short fence through to the next road into the shed. Later we heard that lots of people had seen it happening, from behind their curtains, silently willing them on.

Mr Boomgaard never admitted that he must have seen the two lads taking the bike, for fear of repercussions. As it was, the soldier was beside himself with fury, and could have arrested them both, but for the fact that he ran so hard and far to try and locate his bike, and we could only assume that he was out of puff and could not be bothered to go back to the gravestone yard. Mr Boomgaard never heard any more about the incident, but Beekie never sang so loud again, and we missed his cheerful songs.

Of course that machine was never seen in one piece again. It was obviously demolished for spare parts, in which case everyone could benefit from such a daring escapade. Thus the next week, Willy's old rusty bike, which had cut off rubber tyres from an old worn out car tyre, came riding by with two fantastic air tyres on his rusty wheels, Willy presiding loftily on top.

And the rag and bone man suddenly had a red, white and blue light on the front of his hand cart, and as he shouted his chant, we saw him wink at Beekie, and point to where, if you looked closely, you could still see the little swastika under the thin paint.

Henkie down the road, all of a sudden had a new soft posh saddle on his bike, while his Mum had a brake fitted to her pram, in which she proudly wheeled her latest offspring.

The Girl Who Saw Too Much

Lieve Papa en Rien,   July 1942

Today we saw the Rag and Bone man with his horse and cart, the horse did a big plop plop on the road and Mr Bieze scooped it up into his bucket for his garden. It's not very nice but he says it does marvels for his carrots.

Are you wearing a woollen, great coat, Papa? Mrs Vreedenoord knitted a navy blue coat for me, and Mum lined it with the silk of her skirt, so soft and warm.

Frans got some food for us from the farmers again and we keep the milk cool buried in the ground behind the shed.

We miss you, Daddy, if you can come home we will have a party Mum says.

Love from us all
Mientje xxxx

Helmi Wolff

Dear Papa + Rie

Tonight it was Thunder + lightning after all the warm weather, I saw the lightning forked down and crashed with the thunder clap, I got a bit scared, and I ducked under the table with Dicky, Mum took down the gleaming tin Pot with a plant called Star of Bethlehem from the window seat. She said don't get frightened, I think the angels are moving the furniture.

Dear Pappa,
Today I saw the rag + bone man with his horse + cart. The horse did a big flop plop on the road, and mr. Stiemer dink scooped it up into his bucket, it's not very nice I think, he said his carrots like it, well I don't. Are you weaving a woolen coat Papa, I have a nice blue one, that mrs. .... knitted for me, Mum, lined it with silk, from her skirt, so soft + warm. Frans has got some food from the farmers, for us again, we keep the milk cool, burried behind the shed. We miss you Daddy, come home soon, love from us all
Mientje xxx

The Girl Who Saw Too Much

A Story Mum Told

A regular visitor was Tante Hilda, who was a very large lady. She owned a sewing machine shop in Apeldoorn's High Street, and she had a blonde daughter called Ada, who was twice my age, and was not at all interested in my childish play. She only wanted to sit still and listen to her mum.

What could I do in the meantime? I sat down too; after all, it showed politely that I enjoyed their company, but I found them such dull people, that I started to fidget. Mum noticing my boredom, thought she'd spice it up a little, so when asked by Ada, "Well how did you meet your husband then?" she told them this story.

"Well…" she said! Now I was riveted, as I had never even doubted that they had not known each other forever and ever. "It was like this, you see…" A bit of a pause and three pairs of eyes and ears pointing her way expectantly. She started again. "Frans and I lived next door to each other in a flat, two storeys high, where he lived with his mother, and I lived with mine."

Oh now it gets complicated. Mother must mean her mother! Ah yes Grandma! Got it. "Well," she went on, "he used to hear me play the piano and listened to it. He liked it very much and thought I must find a way of meeting this lady. So one day he called, and when Mother opened the door, he said shyly, 'I have some millet for your parrot, Mrs Nieuwstraten.'

"'Oh well,' came the reply, 'you had better come in, and see if our cockatoo likes it.'

"Millet in hand he followed her up the stairs. Once upstairs he forgot to feed the bird, as he spotted me, the apparent object of his exercise.

"Later he told me that he was so bowled over that he forgot everything else. Well he was asked to have a cup of tea, and it was obvious that Mother liked the look of this rather brave, young man, and quite dandy too, with his fashionable walking cane like that politician Disraeli, and fashionable hat worn at a jaunty angle; and that is not to say what I thought about him either!"

Aunt Hilda gave a roar. Ada joined in. I thought I'd better give a chuckle too, but I was fascinated, a whole new light went up for me, and I was already planning the next episode in our Mother's and Father's game with Vicky.

"Well," said Mum. "He really was so good looking and clean, and he had only fallen in love with the music, so there was something we had in common." Then she went on. "After introductions I found my voice to ask what instrument he liked most."

"Well of course the piano," he said.

"And do you play and instrument yourself, Frans?" she went on to ask.

"Ah yes I play the violin!"

Oh, I thought, I bet he had to learn it yet, that is why we didn't know that he played until their Silver Wedding Anniversary. I started dreaming a little, but I had noticed how pleased Mum always was to see him all dressed up with his shiny boots and felt spats over them. Yes I thought, Mum always liked that a lot, and I think she started to miss that when he had to work hard to feed so many hungry mouths.

He wore a cap when he used to work for a large transport company called Wiekin. This was like a train driver's cap and it got just as greasy and dirty. Mum used to say, "Oh Man, give me that cap, so I can wash it." But it kept him warm and happy on the long journeys over the Pyrenees Mountains to fetch and deliver oranges, with this first early type of articulated lorry. And thus he would say; "Oh no, wife, this cap took me a long time to get, so much work into it. I can't have you wash that out of it now can I?" He never wore it indoors of course!

Helmi Wolff

A Story Dad Told Us in All Its Glory

A handsome chappy was our Dad, when he left school, already fourteen years old.

He felt ready to tackle a job and make some money. He had a few jobs, after which, he and his friend managed to get a lift with a transport company, who went all the way as far a Ghent in Belgium. It was a great adventure. They slept anywhere they could, and relished the unknown.

But the money did not last very long, and they had to get a lift back. His mother had been worried stiff, even though they had told her what they were up to. "You need to find a proper job, Frans, you have to pay your way. I can't feed you for nothing boy!" He had a great idea. "I will ask Mr Reeman with that fantastic car, called an '*Hispano-Suiza*', and with a bit of luck I'll see the inside of that one." That would be just what he hoped for. Mr Reeman liked the look of him, and they got on well.

After working there for a few months, his boss said, "Wolff, you have that car gleaming. I saw my wife using it for a looking glass the other day, before she got in. You do a great job, but… I saw you trying to start it the other day, and what is more, you did!" Dad knew he was not supposed to do that, but at the same time he felt quite proud of himself.

No one he knew could start a car, let alone such a big one. He could boast about that a bit, but he never went out to meet other people, and his Mum would not have approved.

"Well what are we going to do with you?" his boss asked, whilst looking at him sharply.

"I could learn," proffered Frans, and so it was that he watched 'Jo' the proper chauffeur, every time he stopped and started, or did anything to do with driving.

That chauffeur was a bit sloppy, and forgot many times to lock the car, which was just what Frans hoped for. Unbeknown to him, his boss watched him manoeuvre the car precisely and carefully. Presently he came out of his house and stood in front of the car. He knew that Frans could stop immediately.

Highly embarrassed but still looking smart and sharp, Frans opened the car door and his boss got in. "So, you do a very good job," he said. "Would you like to be the new chauffeur, Frans?" Amazed but overjoyed he replied, "Yes please, I would take complete care of the car, and keep it clean and shiny as well."

"We'll see about that, Frans, but first you need to have your livery suit made to your size, and of course there is more to the job, so you have to learn a lot still. In the meantime you get on with your job and learn, there are a few more problems to be ironed out yet."

That evening when he told his mother of his proposed promotion, she could not believe it, and neither could he! Life went on for what seemed to him a long time, before the day came to try on his suit and cap.

In the meantime, there were some unusual jobs all of a sudden, but they made a welcome break.

"Well now, Frans," his boss teased him. "How are you with money?"

"Money?" Surprised by that question, he started explaining what he gave his mum for his keep, but said that he saved the rest.

"Oh, what for?"

"To buy a car of my own, I will be seventeen soon. I could take my mother about, and maybe do some taxi work."

"Well you will be alright then, taking today's takings to the bank, Frans," he said. "Go on your bicycle and take this pack, guard it with your life, and get a receipt from the bank clerk."

Frans tied the pack round his neck and set off on his bicycle over the long bridge of Rotterdam. Look out, a car was swerving. Frans tried to avoid it; he did, but he fell, and what is more the bag with money split and fell down the side of the bridge and down the slopes, towards the water.

What a calamity, fast as lightning he ran after it, scrambled a lot and apparently got every coin back safely into his pockets this time. The bank clerk counted the sum and it all was there.

Pfffffffff that was a near miss, his boss got to hear about it later, and trusted him all the more for it.

"Right now," said his boss, "I have seen you get about in the car, so now you can give me a ride round the town, and we'll see how you do! Old Joe has left, so, if you are all right, that job is yours."

A very satisfied boss got out of the car, on their return, after Frans had backed the 'Hispano-Suiza' neatly into its garage. Mr Reeman beckoned him over, to introduce him to his wife, who had the main use of the car, being driven about endlessly, as she liked to ride and be seen in the *splendid jalopy*.

Mrs Reeman was a rather retiring lady, who liked everything done for her. Her husband waited on her with her tea, whilst he asked her if there was anything else she wanted, to which she just nodded and he knew to put the cushion straight behind her back.

Frans watched this with interest, and thought, perhaps she will learn a thing or two as well. He was introduced to her as the new chauffeur; she looked him up and down, before asking him to turn round slowly, after which she sort of snorted. "Of course dear," said Mr Reeman, "he will have his new livery suit and shoes on." There was no reply from her, and the interview was over.

"Tomorrow morning after coffee time, she will take her seat in the back, and you will have to see she is comfortable and bow as you open the door for her." 'Yes boss,' Frans thought, I will have to speak to her to ask her if she needs anything.

Turning up sharply before time, he shone up the car again before his first official job. And after what seemed a long wait, the lady stood by her front door. Frans manoeuvred the car closely to her, got out and opened the door for her, bowing low. She waited a minute at least before she attempted to get in the car. "Adjust the cushions," she commanded.

She wanted to go shopping. "Wait here until I return."

"Yes, me lady." There were so many stops and starts. "Stop here." *Stop, stay, start. Stop, stay start.* Up and down the High Street, forward and backward for hours. Every time, lackeys bringing more and more boxes and bags into the car. Frans started to feel uneasy, but he helped her into the car and did everything he was told, to the letter.

Up and down the High Street, again and again. Frans got quite sickened with this showy lady. But this routine continued day after day, and Frans dreamed of motoring off into the countryside with the beautiful machine. More and more disgruntled with such stunted distances made worse by the domineering person in the back, he could take no more.

So… One day chauffeuring Mrs Reeman on her shopping spree along the High Street, and being asked for the umpteenth time to stop, start, go, forward and backward again, he turned round and looked at her, and said, "ME LADY, I expect you have learned by now, to drive yourself? I need to have a short walk." At which he got out of the car to walk, back to his boss.

He knew that surely he would have lost his job. He felt guilty, but relieved, and very worried, having left the boss's wife sitting in the car in the parking place.

Mr Reeman saw him coming and looked worried in case something drastic had happened. He came out to meet him in the courtyard, and Frans told him what had happened. There was a stunned silence, while the boss looked at him unbelievingly foxed.

An enormous grin spread across his face from ear to ear. He broke out in to a howl of laughter, and then seemingly trying to stop himself, tried to look sternly at Frans, who had been absolutely amazed at the reaction. And said, "Now, Wolff, that was not the plan, but by heck I've never had the guts to do that."

Frans's face must have been a mixture of amazing emotions, and he remembers having to wipe his nose! "So," said the boss. "You get back like the dickens to where you left her and bring her home. Go on run, boy!"

Showing real remorse at leaving her there, under a torrent of scolding, he got back and bowed deeply with every apology for being so long on his so called short walk.

The weeks went by, and Frans became almost a friend servant to Mr Reeman, always polite and considerate, working hard for his boss, becoming more proficient by the day.

The day came, that he was called into the office. "Sit down, Wolff," said Mr Reeman. "How are you doing with your savings?" he asked. Surprised, Frans replied that he had saved steadily all this time, and by now had accumulated the princely sum of 17 guilders.

"So," his boss went on again, "do you still want to buy a car?"

Looking flushed by now he replied, "Oh yes, sir!"

"Well," stumbled his boss, looking a little moved. "The Hispano-Suiza is now for sale."

Stunned, Frans considered, was he offering? Could he be right in thinking that he could possibly buy this fantastic car? "You have saved enough," the boss went on, "and I know you would treat the car with respect. I have observed you closely, and I can recommend your taxi services to friends of mine."

It was a lot to take in, but aglow, he felt jubilant and could hardly contain his joy.

And this is how Dad's taxi service was born.

Helmi Wolff

An Old Dutch Gin Bottle for Warmth

It stayed bitterly cold and our bedrooms were like ice boxes. There was no heating in the house other than the big range in the kitchen, where the warmth was everyone's friend. We all huddled together there in the evenings sitting close to each other to watch the sparks from the thin slithers of wood that Frans had just cut, with a blanket or coat round our knees.

I loved the cosiness of it when we had what pancakes Mum could produce from whatever we had to make them with. We often had savoury ones, in which little sprigs of dried herbs from the garden gave it some flavour, and for pudding pancakes with sweet beetroot syrup, lovely stodgy food to fill you up.

Just to bring some more cheer we played colour magic, or housie housie, with which I seemed rather lucky.

"Ah no I don't believe it," Hannie said, "she has won again." It was once a week that Hannie came to see us for a whole day.

We walked Freddie together, or did a project like cutting out pictures which she had brought from her job where she lived with the ladies she worked for, in their big house. We made a lovely collage or a stick up house picture, and sometimes we looked through her clothes, from which she could make something nice and new for me to wear.

Mum kept the range glowing to warm us, and kept the pan and kettle boiling, not only to drink some sweetness but also to roast a sort of brown powder which tasted a bit like cocoa, to fill up our conies as we called them.

These were old Dutch brown stone gin bottles, of which we had a few. Not that the gin flowed freely in our house but, when Father was still home, he did sometimes say, "A little nip to keep body and soul together." And Mum used to make a sort of sloe gin with berries soaking for a year in a stone pot to be used for Christmas or New Year's Eve.

The conies were a great comfort in the icy beds, wrapped in two old woollen socks, so as not to burn ourselves. "Can I have two, Mum?" I asked.

"Well yes as it is frosty again." Cuddling round one was great but it always rolled to the sides of the narrow bed.

Mum put them into the beds to air. One at the top and one at the bottom, for our feet. I tried to keep still so it would not roll out on to the floor. Easier said than done, with my red swollen itchy toes due to chilblains. We all had those, in fact Mum's chilblains were the worst and had bitten right down to the flesh making them red raw. They not only covered her toes but also her heals and ankles.

Once a week we all had to attend the Juliana Hospital to have the bandages taken off the weeping sores, to replace them with fresh new ones. This was a very painful process as a lot of the old wet skin came off at the same time, and even though the nurse, who had that unenviable job, was very gentle and kind, to give us all a little peppermint afterwards, I was still frightened of the pain beforehand, and I was shy to show my slightly inwards pointing left foot.

To make matters worse, my special measured left boot was tight and to release it, was a howling matter by itself, and the performance was made worse, because it was done in the packed waiting room, to save time once our turn came.

One little girl who sat next to me leaned over close to my ear and said, "I won't cry when they take my shoe off because I'll do it myself see?" I was amazed to see that she had a very strange foot, which later was explained to me as a clubfoot. It seemed a lot wrong, to me, to have to get into a club for your foot.

Helmi Wolff

Lieve Papa en Rien Nov 1943

We have 32 rabbits, I counted them. Wim caught them, I don't know how he does it, but he can run very fast, one I saw has a sore leg, I hope it gets better. Frans and Wim made cages with chicken wire in the shed for them. I have to feed them and get lots of dandelions and chickweed, but Wim gives them something else a sort of gritty flour I think, he says they are for Christmas, maybe we dress them up pretty for that.

He also gave us another little piglet. Frans hammered a pen to keep him in; it is almost half the shed really with straw and plenty of sawdust from sawing the logs. I have to collect slops and peel from the neighbours round the block in our old pram.

I went to everyone but no one had much to give and they all wanted some of our piggy, surely he is not going to lose his bristles for their brushes?

I think he has grown a bit already and he likes it when I talk to him. I told him not to make so much noise squealing. Do you have any animals there, Papa? I must do my homework now, love to you both.

Mientje

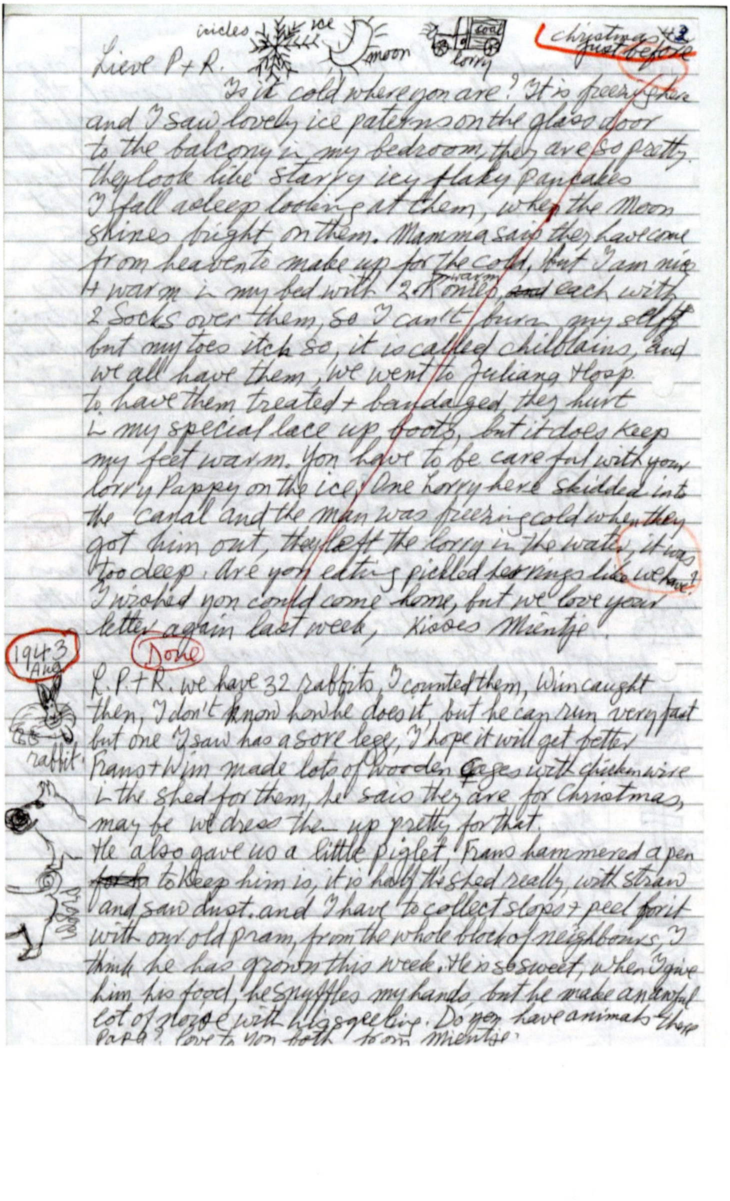

The Girl Who Saw Too Much

[Handwritten letter on lined paper with small drawings in the margins — icicles, moon, lorry, rabbit, piglet. Annotations in red: "christmas just before", "1943 Aug", "Done", "rabbit".]

Lieve P + R,

Is it cold where you are? It is here and I saw lovely ice patterns on the glass door to the balcony in my bedroom, they are so pretty, they look like starry icy flaky pancakes. I fall asleep looking at them, when the moon shines bright on them. Mamma said they have come from heaven to make up for the cold, but I am nice + warm in my bed with 2 Kruiken, each with 2 socks over them, so I can't burn my self, but my toes itch so, it is called chilblains, and we all have them. We went to Juliana + loop to have them treated + bandaged, they hurt in my special lace up boots, but it does keep my feet warm. You have to be careful with your lorry Pappy on the ice, one lorry here skidded into the canal and the man was freezing cold when they got him out, they left the lorry in the water, it was too deep. Are you eating pickled herrings like we have? I wished you could come home, but we love your letter again last week. Kisses Mientje

L.P. + R. We have 32 rabbits, I counted them, Wim caught them, I don't know how he does it, but he can run very fast, but one I saw has a sore leg, I hope it will get better. Frans + Wim made lots of wooden cages with chicken wire in the shed for them, he said they are for Christmas, maybe we dress them up pretty for that.

He also gave us a little piglet, Frans hammered a pen to keep him in, it is half the shed really, with straw and saw dust. And I have to collect slops + peel fruit with our old pram, from the whole block of neighbours. I think he has grown this week, He is so sweet, when I give him his food, he snuffles my hands, but he makes an awful lot of noise with his squealing. Do you have animals there Papa? Love to you both from Mientje

Helmi Wolff

Traditional Dutch Midnight Christmas Dinner

Traditional Dutch Midnight Christmas dinner was always served on Christmas Eve at midnight, by which time we were all very hungry.

Mother and Hanny had laid the table for eight people, as we were allowed to invite our best friend, or other family who may not be having a special midnight feast. Hanny invited her strong boyfriend, Frans the second.

Our Frans asked Johan to join us, as his parents were so elderly, that they went to bed earlier, as if this night was not really special. My friend Vicky was too young to come over at night-time, and her mum and Gran with whom she lived celebrated their own anyway.

On our Christmas Eve walk we had all picked small branches of pine and holly in the woods.

"Oh look," said Han, "these little lark and pine cones are so sweet; we could paint them white with a bit of stiff starch."

"There is some lime whiting left," offered Mum, "you can use that." We all painted little streaks of whiting onto the green.

"It looks just like snow," said I. Frans found a bit of silver lacquer left over from his bike painting, and Mum tore a red farmer's hanky into ribbons for some small bows.

Wim had brought us a dead rabbit but I never saw that.

He seemingly could catch them so fast, that he had enough to peddle round friends and the neighbours.

The table looked so inviting and Hanny's boyfriend could hardly wait for the moment of tasting. Frans and Jo busied themselves in the shed until the time, while Han and I were trying to help in the kitchen. Mum looked steamed up: all red in the face. I thought if only she could stay this colour, it suited her.

By now, it was 11:30 at night and everything was ready. "Go and get spruced up now you two, I will do the same, be quick, we don't want anything to get cold." Our pretty dresses were laid ready and all we had to do was give our face a rinse and comb our hair, but of course Han had to do a lot more, what with her nail varnish and lipstick. We all came down the stairs together, looking in happy surprise at each other. Mother said, "Han, you look great with that little lace bolero over your blue dress."

We entered the dining room together. There was a stunned silence, until the boyfriend whistled loudly in appreciation, "Well," said Frans, "that is magic, 'the three graces' have appeared." Shyly I got to my chair and took care not to crease my dress. Jo said, "Wait till you get to be eighteen."

Well why, I thought, I am eight now and a long way to go! But I realized he was trying to be nice. Oh boys can be so clumsy, they can't help it.

We had our places marked with a little picture Frans had drawn of us all in Christmas colours. It was so very exciting.

By the time Hanny and Mum brought in the steaming hot dishes, we were positively drooling over the wonderful aroma and smells emanating from the very special food. Freddy, for whom the smell of food became too much, had started to run about excitedly, but was told to, 'sit and wait'. Well that was just impossible, so he grunted and shot out of the door momentarily, only to reappear, nose in the air, looking at us so sorry for himself, that Mum bent down and gave him a lovely piece of the rabbit gristle.

The festival atmosphere exuded from everyone. Mum sat down and said we will pray first now, and give thanks for this wealth of goodness. It was really hard for us to sit still with our hands folded, and our eyes closed.

It was a very moving prayer for Father and Rien to be safe and together, and also for the terrible war to end and for so many who were suffering, and more. It did seem to take an eternity to me, but still, I did feel the same as Mum about it all.

At last we started, Frans, being the oldest male in the family, had to carve the rabbit. The large meat plate was handed round, for everyone to take a small portion, so that seconds could go round again.

Then came the wonderful gravy which Mum had made from our few home-grown onions and thickened it with some mashed potato. The vegetables were carrots, which I had pulled in old Mr Bieze's kitchen garden two weeks before, and which Mum had kept fresh in wet sand.

The cabbage was complemented with different herbs from the garden, but I knew that there were also a few dandelion leaves, (which I had picked for Wim's rabbits in our shed). The potatoes were everyone's favourite. They had been rolled in 'saltpetre' from the abattoir, with the skin left on, and then dry roasted in the range oven making them nice and crunchy.

It was a magnificent feast, and for once we were able to actually fill our tummies until full. We thought Mother really deserved a big thank you for this clever cooking.

Hanny led the singing, being the equivalent of *'Oh! She's a jolly good fellow,* for she's a jolly good fellow, for she's a jolly good fellow ow, ow, ow: and so say all of us'. "Well," said Mum, "I had a bit of help you know, but I believe it is time for some games now."

'Pin the donkey's tail', was first. Hanny was blindfolded and turned round and round until she was dizzy and then given the cardboard tail to pin anywhere near its rear. By now she had no idea where that could be. She tried to pin it on Frans who scolded her jokingly, with, "You should know where the donkey's backside is by now!"

Eventually Mum guided her hand and she pinned it in the right place.

We all had a turn and yelped each time someone got it right. *'Nelson's eye'* was next, I didn't like that, as it was gruesome and yucky, nor did I like the sinking ship as you got a wet sponge on your head when you discovered the boat. I remembered it from Liesje's party. But I loved black, green, red or blue magic. I was good at that, and could get it right often. It was a good job that we had all had a sleep in the afternoon. Even then, it was amazing that the excitement lasted well into the small hours of the night.

In the kitchen further delicacies were being prepared on the range. Mum was making some bread pap with beet syrup and also a lot of little pancakes with the same syrup. It was amazing that we were hungry again, but everything was eaten, and I don't remember being carried up to my bed but I woke up the next morning so surprised that the party was over.

Helmi Wolff

Tiddlywinks

One night when I was home alone with Frans, we were sitting at the dining room table, playing Tiddlywinks, but he had to concentrate on his homework from school, which was not easy.

"What is it?" I asked.

"Algebra," he said.

"What's that?"

"You wouldn't know, so be nice and quiet, Mientje."

"Oh." No clue as to what his algebra meant, but he was frowning and sighing, whilst he was writing in his book, funny squiggles and other bits, well what is an eight-year-old to do. I knew I had to think of a game of sorts: a family of tiddlywinks Jahhh!

Every counter that jumped onto the right line got tasted, yes the purple tasted like blackberries. A bit more jumping, and the yellow was good, that had an apple flavour, the red was red currants, but suddenly I choked, amidst horrendous coughing and choking, I felt faint. Frans rushed over, grabbed me by the legs and held me upside down, slapping me hard on my back. Suddenly the silly red counter jumped out of my throat.

Tears streamed down my face. Frans was shocked too, "What you do that for, you silly girl?" I was so shocked that I forgot to cry, he was trying to be extra kind stroking my hair, he said, "Never do that again, Mientje," and then in a very stern voice, "Silly girls!"

"No I won't," I said in a very small still choking voice.

I don't think he got much of those funny sums done after that, but Mother got to hear about it on her return. She said, "I know a much better game we can play with a blunt knife on a round bread board."

She had some little love hearts sweets in her little silver box. Now she said, "I will start to spin the knife, and **Ohhh** where does it stop? It points at a button, what a shame, I don't get anything for that. You have a go now." I spun the knife and *ohhh* it stopped at a pink love heart. "Now you can eat that," she said one more time before bed, and then we play again tomorrow.

The next day I had to help Mum to dry the dishes after supper. She said, "You are good at that and a great help today. Tomorrow we will start to spring clean again and I know you will help me a lot."

Frans had gone out flying his homemade kite with his friends, I wanted to go out too, but it was too near bed time for me, still he came home quite soon and said, "Look I can do the crab, Mien." He crawled backwards in a crab posture, around on the floor and table, crooning, "Come on you can sit on my tummy and I'll be like a spider." I wasn't too sure but wobbled along anyway.

He was so clever, he could stand on his hands upside down, and "I can walk like that too," he said and he did! Mother and I were well impressed.

It was the Sunday evening meal. I loved the time when all four of us sat around the table and Mum brought in the hot steaming stamp pot, usually made with whatever vegetables and potatoes there were, and maybe some meat or sausage, which always smelled so good. But before we could eat there was the prayer of thanks and the short bible reading.

Yes dinner times were something else, as it was the time to see each other, but not to talk when grownups were speaking, and to wait sitting up with poker straight backs and hands folded on the table, until served our portion of nourishment.

By then some of us had been swallowing our saliva for ten minutes, smelling the food in the big pan.

I loved the interval between eating and the next bible reading, when we could converse to our heart's delight. "How was your day?" Hanny said. Everyone had a story, sometimes I made one up if I had nothing exciting to say, but it was usually too fantastic to be real. Mostly Frans talked about school. He had to do so many difficult tests, and Mum said she would try to see someone to help him.

Hanny talked about her nice little boyfriend, but said that he was always busy doing homework too. I knew that she liked him a lot. She told me that they would meet at church time when she was supposed to be there. Instead she asked me to tell her about the sermon etc., so I tried to remember the reading and the psalms for her in case Mum would ask. I felt important and chummy doing that and I never told on her.

I told her that Frans could walk on his hands and like a crab too. "Oh yes," she said, "so can my friend he can walk down the street like that."

"Oh yes?" said Frans, "well who is he then?"

"I'm not telling you."

I started to dream a bit of when Dad was still with us. He did a trick with a little plank, and got me to stand on his hands. He'd help me up and then a scarf was tied around my eyes so I could not see anything. Supporting me with his other hand, I was lifted towards the ceiling. Mum was shouting, "Careful, careful, she'll hit the ceiling." Suddenly I hit what I thought was the ceiling, oh, I cried, everyone laughed. I wobbled, was I flying: I was flying?

The scarf was removed and to my chagrin I saw the small plank that Frans was holding above my head, ah that's how it was done then.

The Girl Who Saw Too Much

I was elated but also disappointed when I knew and understood the trick, as I'd been bragging to Vicky that I could fly to the ceiling.

Oh I was missing my Dad so much.

Well by now the ceiling was to make a quite different impression on me, as spring cleaning had arrived again. Yes little did I know that I'd be washing that very ceiling the next day.

Mother had saved some of the suds from the washing in her wooden barrel washing machine apparatus for the purpose of the big wipe clean. The small step ladder served very well for reaching the corners of the room, and since I was light and the ladder flimsy, I got to go up whilst Mum reached up to give me the clean soaking rag, rinsed out every time in a bucket of slightly grey suds.

I slopped the sodden rag along the ceiling forward and backward. Mum said, "Don't forget that bit and that smear etc."

Dad had laid on electrics with whatever wire and tools he had, and the connections were not water proof and insulation tape had been put everywhere to make ends meet literally, along the dado rail near the ceiling. Mum had never been up there and anyway electric power was like magic to her.

Suddenly I got a big jolt and was knocked sideways making me fall into Mother's arms. I was stunned, and it was a total puzzle to all of us as to what had happened there. The bucket of suds had capsized; everything was swimming, and so was my head. Luckily the voltage was very low, only enough to power a small bicycle light bulb. However, that was the end of the cleaning for the day. "Well done!" said Mum!

Helmi Wolff

Lieve Papa en Rien   June 1944

I like the syrup beet root sauce Mama makes it is so nice and sweet I get a spoonful after I have had my levertraan (cod liver oil) that is so horrible that I got an extra spoonful of syrup but Mama said that if you want the last drop out of the can, the lid will fall on your nose. I tried once but my nose was fine.

I saw a swan flying in Orange Park he was beautiful, first he ran so fast on the water and then he took off but he did not go far. School is now only on the playground, because of the German soldiers having to sleep in our school on straw, we must not go in there. So we do our homework and show it to Miss in the playground, then she gives us new work and keeps the other over night, to put red marks on if it is wrong.

I have a big bong on my forehead because I trod on the rake in the shed and the stick clapped on my head, just like the one when I walked into the school door. There is not much food for the pig now.

Lots of love Mientje

The Girl Who Saw Too Much

Frans and his cowboy band.
The straw matting of the shed is showing.

Helmi Wolff

Goose Eggs

As I have said more responsible jobs came my way now I was nearly nine years. Mother had heard that a farmer near the canal was selling goose eggs. "So, Mien," she said, "you can go on your bicycle to buy some. Here is the money in this little purse," which was put in a large cloth bag to hang on the handlebars of our full-sized bike that used to belong to Hanny.

It had solid rubber tyres, cut from old worn lorry tyres. The saddle had been lowered as much as possible and the paddles had thick wooden platforms screwed on to them so I could reach the blocks.

"Don't break the eggs, Mien," Mum called after me.

"No I won't, Mum." It was a long way on the sand roads, and I peddled fast, through the sleepy village of Apeldoorn to the canal. I was tempted to look in the shops on the big roads, especially one huge shop which had a display of beautiful crockery, and all the same pattern too.

Cor, I thought, not like our enamel mugs and chipped plates. In a dream I peddled on, thinking of whom I would invite if I had such lovely tableware to show off with. But of course I would be married all in white lace, frothy as the white blossom on our pear tree, and I could have a beautiful horse drawn carriage, like that song, 'a rich lady, and a bride groom', of course.

Now why did my school master Mr Wonderful's face cross my dreamy mind?

Ah daydreams, look out, the canal farm was not much further. There was a real country smell to guide me.

The Girl Who Saw Too Much

Mum had said, just follow your nose, and yes, that was it, the farmhouse guarded by a huge ferocious looking dog barking in a vicious way.

Timidly I opened the gate, upon which the dog was called back, and at that, a lot of quacking gaggling geese came running at me. The noise was overwhelming. I started running back to my bike, and wondered how I would ever be able to ring the bell. Suddenly the farmer's wife appeared looking at me. She shouted over the din of the geese, "Come on in, young un, they won't hurt yer!"

One goose pecked my skirt and caught my bum. "Ouch," I shouted.

"Shoo, shoo," she said, shooing them away, as she lead me to a large shed. "Here you are, young un, I will put some of these eggs in yer bag shall I?"

"Yes please." I gave her the money, but she said it was too much, and gave me almost half of it back. "Oh thank you and goodbye," I shouted, already out of the gate and on my bike again.

It was easier said than done peddling with one hand supporting the enormous eggs, and the other on the handlebars, I had to steer and ring my bell all with one hand now. Peddling as smoothly as possible, holding the bag away from my legs and the pedals, I got home without breaking any at all.

Mum was so pleased, and I thought I would show her a little trick for fun. So, as I was walking towards her, I swung the bag round my head. She shouted out, "No!" Too late did I realize that I was now under the cross pole for beating the carpets.

The bag hit it, a great egg mass fell on my head. I stood dripping and shocked. "Ohh," Mum scooped eggs off me and caught most of the rest before they hit the ground. I rescued the bag with lots of **goo** inside. We picked out the eggshells and put the rest into a big bowl. That evening we had a lovely big omelette and pancakes galore.

"Mm, Mien, you should do that more often," Hanny said after being told the egg story. A lot of laughter followed, but I was not happy with all that jollity at my silly trick.

"It would have been a good trick," I defended, "had that stupid pole not been there." More laughter, oh this is maddening!

Even Mrs Backer across the road had heard about my goose egg fiasco. Mr Backer was told too, and he was a joker, always trying to tease me in an innocent way but still able to rock my little boat.

His usual approach was to have me sing a song for a sweet, after which he would sing a little ditty, usually made up to suit the occasion. Well this time he had a different one, and he could not wait to recite it. I was surprised that he did not ask me to sing first, instead of which he got me to stand close to him and started his own, like this:

"WileMien sulleMien had nog nooit de stok gezien,
Met een zwaai raakte hem fraai
En dat was het einde van eier Mien," all in his lugubriously flowing lilting song voice.

In English it goes like this:
Willemien, silly Mien, didn't see the beam
She swung the bag, and hit the stack
And that was the end of egg splashed Mien.

I nearly died of shame, but before I could speak Mrs Baker popped a lovely sweet in my mouth, and said, "Now, now man, you know better than to tease her, come on now, and let off you!" At least he did not do his usual trick of: "Close your eyes, Mien, and put out your hand," as on that other occasion. Not that I would have fallen for that trick. It had been done to death on my sisters too; even Frans fell for it when he was little. Mrs Baker went on to say: "You know that Mientje just had an accident, oh she was so lovely."

Helmi Wolff

Lieve Papa en Rien, **21 Nov. 1943**

Yesterday was Mama's birthday I made some paper roses from the left over parchment of our kite to decorate mama's chair. Frans used the ribbons of his kite as well and Hanny had a pretty hair clip to stick on the top. We did it really early before she got up, she was so surprised and pleased and when she sat on it she said I feel like a proper princess, and she was wearing her best blouse and skirt. You know, blue with yellow squiggles and flowers, so we all sang Happy Birthday to you.

I found a nice piece of wood and Frans helped me to make an Easter cross of it for her. She said she would like to put it next to the photos in her bedroom. Hanny gave her the hair clip but she said it is so lovely that we should both wear it at times. She wore it at the back of the knot in her hair. It looked lovely, and today Hanny is wearing it on the front of her hair.

We had hotpot with carrots and onions for dinner, do you get that there, Papa? I expect you are too busy to come back to us now?

Lots of love Mientje

The Girl Who Saw Too Much

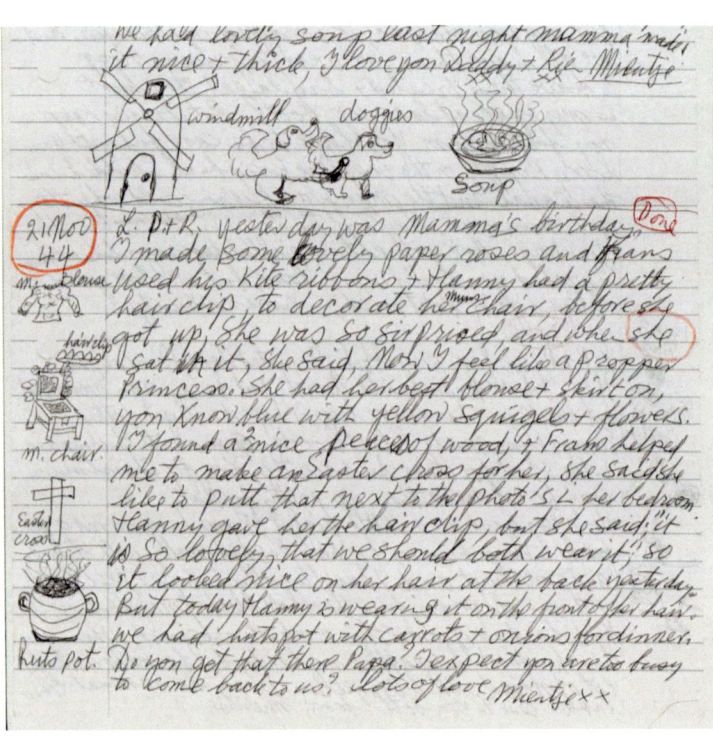

Helmi Wolff

Tienhoven

I was told this story, which is typical of so many, but this is one with variations, to say the least.

My friend Sientje was just seven years old when the whole low lying area of Tienhoven and many surrounding places were flooded. It is a water rich place, now much used for boating and other water pursuits.

Her family along with many had to evacuate to the north of Holland. All children and parents were put on a train, and they headed north. Suddenly the cry went up: 'Bombers coming', the train stopped, everyone had to get out because of the impending danger.

Scrambling for safety a coal bunker was spotted and deemed the best hiding place for them. Sientje's brother, Klaasje, only two years old, started to climb into the black coals, loving it. He was retrieved by his mother, and given a warning but before she had uttered the words the train was bombed severely. Shaking with fright and nerves they stayed in their hiding places until another train was found to take them on the second lap of their journey.

They all looked as black as the ace of spades, but Mother knew what to do. Surely they could not arrive at the waiting families the other end like that. So out came the lemonade bottle she had with her and a hanky was moistened to rub Klaasje and all of them clean. The little fellow cried a bit when she had to put a light pressure on to his face to clean him.

This sparked off the discomfort of an elderly gentleman who could not wait to relieve himself. After wriggling about for a while, he took of his hat, and turning to the back a bit, so no one could see, he proceeded to fill his hat with the warm liquid.

Well what to do with it now; he thought of something, and opening the window as wide as possible, he proceeded to fling the contents out of the running train against the wind, and yes of course, it all splattered back giving everyone a shower. Klaasje was crying again. Once more Mother got out the lemonade bottle and sponged every one down, not a lot left to drink now but then nobody felt thirsty for that lemonade.

Finally they arrived at their destination. Burgerbrug station seemed too small for all the people, but they all got assigned to someone, when suddenly it was noticed that Sientje's sister, Riek, was stippled red. Measles Oh dear! Perhaps they had all got it by now?

No they could not stay for the risk of infection, they had to go back home, but that was impossible. A small hospital was set up and they found that quite a few of them had the measles.

After a few days the word came that Tienhoven was almost dry, they could travel back now on a train again. Sientje remembers that the polder was still under water, which became a great swimming pool with floating bits of wood to climb on. No one thought of the danger of uneven depth, and sharp things or disease. They played and had fun till the meadow was dry enough to let the cows graze there again on the newly grown grass.

Helmi Wolff

The Old Pram

I was so tired and still feeling weak which made my left foot drag a bit as I went through the umpteenth garden gate, calling, **"Any peel or slops for our piggy**, please Mrs Freedenoord?"

It took some time for her to get to the door, as she was not so quick on her feet now. Whilst waiting I looked into her garden to see if there were any weeds I could pull up.

But which were the cabbage and potato plants? I had seen her work at digging and planting, with her poorly feet: better ask first.

"Ah there you are, Mien, well no, I don't peel me tatties any more, Mien. There ain't no slops fir us now, let alone fir yer pig, but yer's welcome to pull up t' dandelions and t' other weeds from t' back garden there, and when yer finished, come in and I'll give e some kruidmous; that's fir yer, mind, not fir t' pig!"

Mrs F. was a kindly old woman, she had always lived on her own, and if she had some knitting wool, could be seen any time standing knitting, knitting at her front gate, knitting, knitting, knitting, and not missing any goings on in the road, or any bit of news, to gossip about to any passing person.

"See now, I've warmed it up fir yer, Mientje, get that down yer, warm yer hands on't cup, yer half famished child," as she fetched a cup of steaming barley and herb broth from the range. I took it gratefully and although it was too hot still, I could not wait to start sipping.

It was warm in that kitchen and very homely with the gleaming Delft Blue tiled surround. The pot with soup broth was bubbling and gurgling on the hob, and the welcoming fire warming me.

The Girl Who Saw Too Much

She scooped a cupful for herself as well, and sat next to me on the little bench. "How's yer Mum now? Her legs was poorly last week, her varicose veins playin up? She had to bandage it, did she? I saw her hobblin' a bit, is she goin' to t'ospital to get it done properly like?"

"I don't know, Mrs F., she got a dog bite, when she was visiting my aunt in the 'Brink laan' last week."

"Oh thas nasty, did it bleed?"

I had never seen Mum's legs bare, the wrinkled stockings she always wore covered them, but I did on this occasion, when I had to hold the pad with the bandage in place, while Mum secured it with the bit of torn sheeting for a bandage, to wind round her poorly leg.

I had been shocked to see the swollen leg with the blood dripping; so I answered, "Yes it was awful Mrs F."

"You lot are in t' wars eh? What with yer brover Frans tripping, when he ran backwards trying to fly his kite, and fallin' he cut his head, so he did, 'ad to 'ave it stitched up in t'ospital, as he been to get it checked out since? Now, child, let's be avin yer, I needs to measure yer. I've got some blue wool and I'll knit yer another coat and 'at! Stand up now, Mientje, oh what a bag a bones yer are." Oh yes I was only too willing, a new knitted coat for me just like Liesje had, it was navy blue wool too!

"Lift up yer arm, Mientje, so as oi can fit the pattern on yer properly like." She made a thorough job of it, which took some time, all the time chatting to me in such a soothing way, that I almost drifted off.

My thoughts strayed back to when I left our house earlier, in an attempt to feed the poor starving animal. With the desperate squealing of piggy bellowing in my ear, as it always did. I had dreamed that he would break loose and trample down his flimsy pen, run away and get lost in the surrounding woods of Apeldoorn.

But then this morning as piggy pots snuffled my hand, and I fed him a hand full of grass and weeds picked alongside the banks of the Sprenge Brook, I promised to get him a better meal, collected from the neighbourhood of our small village.

On my way home I felt much better, and especially now that the old pram was partly filled with fresh greens and Mr Bieze's worm eaten carrots, which he let me pull as well.

I was smiling to myself, mission accomplished I thought, piggy would be able to fill his tum-tum this time.

Freddy ran up to greet me in the road, jumping with elation at seeing me. I patted him, but told him that this was all for piggy. His tail dropped; *did that dog understand?*

Wheeling the old pram up the drive and to the back of the house I could see a lot of sawdust in the entrance of the shed. Frans was sawing the thick logs he cut from a dead tree. "Ah just what I need, Mien, a heavy weight, to hold the wood down while I saw."

"Yes but I need to give piggy this first."

By then the din of the squealing was deafening, and Freddy got so excited, yapping almost melodiously whilst jumping at the pram and me. "Down boy, down now boy, good boy."

He was such a lovable little character, very adventurous, a bit naughty at times but such a nice little cuddle when you needed one.

"Oh there you are, Mientje, I got a bit worried, you were such a long time." "Yes Mrs Fredenoord is going to knit a coat and hat for me, Mum, and she gave me some hot Kruidmoes."

I clambered on to the rickety sawing horse, which was swaying dangerously from left to right and back, in fast succession. "You're not sitting on the log properly," Frans said, he could hardly control the dangerous contraption.

"Sit still, Mien, will you?"

"I am, I am."

"Oh it's no good, I suppose you can't help being a girl eh?" Bah!

The Girl Who Saw Too Much

Helmi Wolff

Lieve Papa en Rien,   Nov 1944

I don't know what has happened to our piggy pots, he has gone and I don't know where. Wim says wait till you taste him, I don't understand, but I don't have to collect slops and potato peel any more.

All the rabbits are growing big, Wim comes to look sometimes but Frans and I feed them. We have to pick lots and lots of dandelions and other stuff, but they also get some sort of smelly pellets. Frans had to get those from the big windmill.

We have a lot of beans in the cellar all pickled in, and Mum also cooked pears and apples in glass jars. There is no more growing in the garden until next spring, but we got potatoes from a field that had been harvested. Do you have enough to eat Papa? We don't have much but Mum makes pancakes of most things.

The Girl Who Saw Too Much

Our Upside Down Bicycle

We had endured very cold winters before, but this year was the coldest. We had run out of fuel, and had no coupons, to get coal. Even though our coal man, Mr Siemens, was a neighbour, he still could not let us have more fuel than our coupons allowed.

Already we had used the sifted coal bits that were placed in the rough tray to shake hard in the morning, after the ashes were left in the grate. Mum usually plopped the ashes and bits in that tray while Frans or Hanny shook it violently to be left with enough fuel to glow merrily the next evening.

The temperature was twenty-one degrees below zero on this day, dropping even lower at night; it really was bitterly cold. Our thin bodies were not able to sustain our own heat. I had to put a bowl of something in the metal dustbin, but when I tried to open the lid my hand froze to it, stuck fast onto the lid. I yelled, and Mum came running. Frans did what I could not believe: he peed onto my hand while Mum pulled, to free it. I was shocked, and needed to be defrosted near the warm range.

Mr Siemens had already given Frans a sack with rough coal dust which he somehow managed to press into combustible pieces for burning. Mum told him he could have all the pears that hung over his side this year, but he replied, "We already do have those every year!"

Frans and Henkie went down to the woods again to saw and cut more wood for the fire. They always came back with a full load, laden on the little cart that he had made from the wheels of my little tricycle, for which I had not quite willingly forgiven him yet. But it did mean that we got the lion share of all the wood, even if all of it had to be sewn up in our shed on the old swaying saw horse. After which it would be divided to bring almost half of it to Mr and Mrs Masselaar, the remainder of which had to be piled up neatly in one corner of the shed, for some to be dried enough to be cut into kindling wood.

We had to be sparing with everything, but evenings were quite cosy and warm, sitting all together with a blanket over our knees by the glowing range. Every five minutes a very thin slither of kindling was fed into the open little doors to make a bit of flaring flame, enough to see by. It did cast ghostly shadows and dancing lights, I loved to fantasize and play with the dancing shadows and leaping flares of light. Electricity had long been unavailable owing to the destruction of the pylons and the electricity works.

Let's play magic moments – this was a game of ingenuity and luck and you did not have to get up to take part as in black magic or others. Mum managed to fry some potato pancakes on the heat, made with the thin peel that I had collected in the old pram, which had been picked over for the best and then thoroughly washed, grated or stamped finely, and mixed with a little flour and fat if we had it, then fried on the range.

This delicacy was for the last thing at night before bedtime, often with a hot cup of watery sweetened milk, which was prized by us all. If there were more than we needed ourselves we shared this food, often with a neighbour or one of Hanny's friends if it was her day off.

We giggled a lot at everything when stories were told. Freddy wanted to sit between us, when we told even scare stories of escape and other danger, partly with nervous tension or just to keep warm.

Frans put a new bit of kindling into the fire, a spark spat at us and landed on my lap, which was quickly extinguished, but left a hole in the blanket. "Ah well," said Mum. "I was going to make a coat for myself with that old blanket anyway and I could cut round the hole," so that was that!

Hanny asked what had happened to the sort of wind blade mill we had on a tall post in the garden before, that was supposed to give us some electricity, enough for a small light. "Well," said Mum. "We did not have the right connections for it, like Mr Bentsink had, to work it."

Frans had a bright idea, as he now had a red white and blue painted over a dynamo on his bike which fuelled a light running on the rim of the front wheel of his bicycle, (after the German bike episode). "I'll bring in my bike again," said Frans. "We put it upside down, peddle hard, and that will give us enough light with the new dynamo."

The bicycle was brought indoors, and put upside down. "You'll be for it," Hanny scoffed.

"Ah ha," said Frans. "This will be a lot better than the carbide light we tried before." so he proceeded to make himself comfortable with a cushion before lying upside down to peddle like the clappers, to show a glowing light. He and Gerard took it in turns to peddle hard, and voila we had light.

"Can I have a go, Frans?" I asked all excitedly, both of them laughed. "Well?" I questioned.

"Oh go on then." *How ungrateful boys are, I thought.* Trying to reach the pedals was not an option for me. Hanny put three cushions under my back and yes that was better.

Legs akimbo, skirt flapping, I managed to make the wretched pedals go round, but no light. Oh well! Hanny brought in her latest little boyfriend, and not so little either. He was smirking contentedly and went over to lie down under our famed bike. "Watch this," he smirked again, while he made himself comfortable. Wow, he was the best, he nearly made the bike zoom with vibrations, strong powerful legs, the light glowed white, and he nearly pinged the bulb.

"Where on earth did you get that dynamo, Frans?" asked Mother.

"Oh I just found it in some junk at Henkie's shed." A very thoughtful look passed Mum's face, a trifle dubious!

The Girl Who Saw Too Much

Lieve Papa en Rien   **Autumn 1944**

Mum dyed a lovely, silk scarf, red for me, so I could join the junior girl guides. They are all a bit bigger than me, but nice. We sing at the Salvation Army in the choir. One of the older girls is called Janny, and she told me that she likes our Frans. Later I saw Frans talking to her, with his arm around her too! I felt a bit put out, but he just went back to his trumpet playing in the band there.

So I went for a long bike ride with Freddy. He ran along my side all the way, and when we got back he was too tired to eat, so he just slept, and slept.

When are you coming back, Papa? We miss you so much.

Mientje xxx

Helmi Wolff

Tina

We had some Jewish friends in Amsterdam. Mum was very anxious about them after she heard how they had all been rounded up like cattle and driven from their homes, after they had separated the men from the woman and children, (some only sixteen-year-old boys were counted as men and the young girls as women too). Wives, sisters, and children, fathers, brothers and little boys even babies were taken to be stowed into cattle trucks to be taken to Germany, often straight to the death camps.

Of course I would not have known any of that while I was so young, but at school it was talked and prayed about in such a sad way that I think all of us realized that something very nasty and dangerous had happened. It left a deep impression on me when the schoolmaster prayed so fervently for this disaster to be diverted and for all who had seen this barbaric brutality.

It reminded me of the day this had happened to us, when they had taken my Daddy and Rien to march them away from us. I had not seen them since; a great feeling of sadness spread over me. I had such a job holding my tears at bay. It left me with silently screaming in my head, such was the effect of anguish that there was no concentration for work left in me, or in the other children either and we were all excused to leave for home early.

I asked Mum if her friends were among them, she pinked away her tears, turned round and said, "I don't know, love, but I do know that we can try to save Tina. She is a lovely girl and you will meet her later." I was kept busy for the rest of that day so I would not see anyone to talk to.

The Girl Who Saw Too Much

Feeling excited about the visitor, I had no idea of the plan in hand at that time. Many years later I heard that Tina was the daughter of a very old friend who had managed to hide in a dung lorry while the Gestapo raid was happening. She had been totally immersed in dung just keeping her nose above it, breathing with the aid of a hollow bit of twig like a straw.

Another friend (quite an old lady) had collected her in secret to take her to her home in Apeldoorn, from where Frans later collected her, in the evening on his bike. However, this old lady had a son who was a baker. He and his family lived in the same house but downstairs where he had his shop. He was not a kind man.

To make matters worse this man was a 'N S Ber', (Netherlands service burger) which means, someone who was allowed privileges by the German army in exchange for information.

He had openly threatened his mother with collaboration to tell and inform the German army about Tina's hiding place. Thus she was in immediate danger of discovery, and in an effort to help, Mum had agreed to take her in for the moment. She was to be collected by the underground workers to hopefully get onto a submarine, to escape to America as many managed to do with the help of people like my brave mum and many other secret workers.

Frans was a bit jumpy, of course I did not know why, as all that sort of information was kept away from me but evening came and he hooked up the little cart that he had made with the wheels of my tricycle to set off under the cover of darkness. He peddled fast through the small alleyways that he knew so well, so as not to be spotted, as there also was a curfew, to be indoors after dark.

I believe that Tina was hiding in the house ready to go, the moment Frans arrived.

Back home Mother was praying for his safe return with Tina, and after about twenty minutes he was back. Mum ushered Tina into the house. She was trembling with fright and exhaustion. We sat her down in a chair with a warm blanket, and it took a few moments before she could speak. "Thank you," she said, which were all the words I ever heard from her, because, they had hardly got home and unloaded, when a loud banging, on the front and the back door simultaneously, shook us all. Tina sat up rigid and then she half climbed onto the harmonium organ as fast as she could, to jump behind it into the space in the corner of our room.

I saw Mother turning deadly pale, Frans was shaking. Mum held me tight, but the banging and shaking got worse. They were shouting, "Was haben sie dar, Juden shwine hund, Ofnen sie tese ture schwine hund." We had to open the door.

Mum went to the front and opened up, and with that, two soldiers stormed through into the hall, where one of them saw the portrait of Queen Wilhelmina which he smashed with his fist, making it bleed, shouting, "Verukte schwine hund." The other one saw the picture of the Lord's prayer, which then also got smashed, glass splinters and shards everywhere. Shouting, and pushing Mum aside, they moved quickly through the kitchen, knocking over anything in the way, finally getting into the sitting room.

They wasted no time but looked straight behind the organ and saw Tina cowering there.

They yanked her out so roughly, upon which she produced her false identity pass. They looked at it but were not impressed, and started to drag her out of the house, all the time swearing and cursing. As a last desperate attempt Mother said, "Of course, we were all scared and that is why she jumped behind the organ." I will never forget the fear and cold sweat on her poor twisted face, as she was dragged out of our sight.

That night in bed I heard the steam train hiss and blow. I wondered if Tina was on board, and how she was coping with perhaps hundreds of other Jewish people pressed together into a freight train. I pulled the bedclothes over my head so as to shut out the sounds; it was as if the train itself was howling in sad indignation to be used for such a human freight.

I could not hear the sobbing from both Mum and Frans but realized later that the devastating sadness was born by us all.

The next day it was as if the smell of what had happened was still in our nostrils. Was it the smell of fear? It caught in my tender young heart.

Were there going to be awful repercussions? Was Mum going to be arrested next? I sent up a childish prayer to look after Tina. We all looked so ill and weak; maybe they had what they came for, but anything could still happen. I had been to the station once with my little friend Vickie only to be shooed away.

I could not understand that just because the Jewish people wore the lovely Star of David on a yellow armband and also showed that in their shops, that the German soldiers got so nasty about that.

Mum explained to me that they were made to wear these and so be identified by that emblem. Little did I realize then how that evil regime worked, to tighten its grip on all of us even more, and accounted for so many atrocities in Apeldoorn and the surrounding district, let alone in the big towns, where the worst war crimes were committed.

When I asked Mum what would happen to Tina, she looked so sad, but managed to smile, and said, "Tina has gone to a new home, and afterwards she will go to a much better home."

Helmi Wolff

Lieve Papa en Rien   Jan 1944

We don't have much dinner stuff left, but Frans got some dark brown bread and fat bacon and milk from the farmers. Mum is making stamp pot, lovely I am hungry.

I have drawn the cattle train that they took Tina in. I am so sad. We will not know where she is, they came and took her away, she jumped behind the organ and she was so scared, we all were. Mummy is ill and I tried to sit upright but I was ill too. Mum says they have taken her to a new home.

The train in the station is screeching and blowing smoke. I hate to hear it and I cover my head under the blanket. I don't like it Papa, come home soon please we love you so much.

Mientje

Later stories reached us of people jumping overboard in desperation whilst travelling often in open coal trucks. Also of one man who had managed to hide a hand saw on his person, with the intent to saw a hole into the floor of the wagon, so that every time the train stopped at a station, on its long journey to stow even more people onto that train, some could escape, one by one onto the tracks – many only to be seen and shot. But some made it, and got away to the nearest farm and some were lucky enough to get accommodation.

My sister, Nelly, later met one of these people. She was the last to wring herself free through the hole, out of that wagon, but she was still holding onto the rails when the train started rolling. Consequently she managed to flee with crushed hands. She survived to tell my sister this tale. My sister was employed by her, long after the war was over.

The Girl Who Saw Too Much

Beautiful Frost Stars

I looked up at the wood planked sloping ceiling of my little bedroom which was glistening with frost patterns in the moonlight. Ice needles actually hung down from the top ledge there. I marvelled at how water was so strong and brittle when it froze, and it looked as if they were like little Christmas lights that I had seen in a shop once, when the moonbeams hit them.

We had just learned about stalagmites and stalactites in caves, and how they formed over many thousands of years. The teacher had even spoken of millions and billions of years, which was quite incomprehensible to most of us; such a long time, like eternity, they sing about in the church.

I started fantasizing about *floating in a silvery cave*, everything was shiny and light and so fragile. The beautiful ice patterns on the window were beckoning me. I dreamed that I was floating, floating in ice, not feeling cold at all. I don't know how long it lasted but I woke up being violently sick. Somehow I had not digested the meagre little supper at all.

I brought it all up and made such a mess of the bed. Mum came running in and cleaned me up, the entire time saying, "Don't worry, love." I was shivering and shuddering in her arms. She wrapped her old housecoat around me and calmed me down, after which she took me in to her bed and we cuddled up together.

The night had faded into daylight and with it came the realization that I was hardly able to move anything. Half awake and feeling so weak and woozy drifting in and out of consciousness, I was aware of a terrific pain inside my right ear. It seemed to go through my whole head.

Our old doctor came to see me. Only half able to see, I heard him say rather than ask, "Well, Mientje, what have you been up to?" His voice seemed a long way off. I just looked at him and noticed how wrinkly his face was, but his kindly bright blue eyes looked at me, and then he touched the painful side of my head. A silent scream escaped my mouth. Talking to Mum for a while he gave her some medicine for me and left soon afterwards.

Warm oil on a tea spoon was poured into my ear, which soothed it somewhat, but to turn over onto the other side was more than I could muster. It was excruciatingly painful when Mum tried to turn me over. Everything ached so badly, hot sweat was running down my face, fireworks exploded into multiple sparks and even though my eyes were closed, needles seemed to sting me all over, before blackness took me into a different phase.

Crying silently when I awoke, I saw Mum still sitting next to me. She was cradling me in her arms and holding a warm mug of milky stuff, for me to drink. It was ladled into me spoon by spoon, along with lots of coxing, stroking, kissing and other sweet-talk. I had no idea what it tasted like.

The day drifted by, between more medicine and oil being administered into my ear, interspaced with this strange warm drink, which I now know to be thick barley water with some beet syrup mix.

Mum was with me most of the time, and later when Frans came in, he said something like: "Mien, I need you to make a new tail for my kite, I've got all the string and paper."

Later Hanny came to see me too, and sat with me for a while to tell me a spring story about lambs in a field and daffodils blooming. I hardly heard her but somehow it got to my brain, and dosing off again I dreamt of a lovely field full of flowers blooming in the grass and a little lamb gambling about in the sun. I don't know where the dream ended but it felt good and soothing.

At least four days of this half consciousness lasted, and all the time Mum cuddled up with me in her bed, between jobs, and at night.

I felt a bit better, full of medicine. The doctor came again, and that was when I noticed that he had grazed himself on his cheek and forehead. I asked him if it hurt. "Not any more, Mientje," he replied. It was not until after that dreadful war, that I was told what a brave man he was and how he had tried to keep resistance workers hidden in his secret shelter.

After talking again to mum, he left, but the next thing was another ordeal.

Mother had to somehow empty me of faeces, my extended bloated tummy was full of heaped up excrement. It was very unpleasant; a rubber tube was inserted into my already painful rectum, after which lukewarm suds were poured into a funnel slowly filling me up to bursting point. I felt I was going to blow up, but it had the desired result. Oh, it was horrible; this procedure was repeated daily for perhaps a week. I hated to see the large enamel bowl coming in daily laden with tubes and suds.

Doctor came again after a few days and after the customary examination, he talked to mum, and I caught snatches of conversation like: *'yes very sore'*, and *'no not today yet'*, also *'very difficult yesterday'*. Malnutrition was one of the words.

I was given a bath in bed, in a large bowl full of purple stuff, three times a day, big enough for me to sit in. I wondered from where it came, surely lent to us by a neighbour, I thought. Later I realized that this was gentian-violet. It stayed on my skin and inside me, where I had to squeeze the sponge and squirt it into me.

This also went on for a week, and in the meantime I started to feel better, eating broth and bread now. My bony frame was less painful, and I wanted to get out of bed. Mum helped me but there was no way I could stand on my legs, they were like jelly flopping instead of supporting me. She carried me to the window and I noticed that the snow had gone which had been banked up in our road at least three feet high before. I was so glad to be up, but even more thankful to be back in bed. I was a long way from being well yet.

The days were interspaced with school homework, which Frans collected and often sat with me to complete. I tired so quickly to start with, but gained strength as I went along. Hanny came in most evenings, to show me how she had sorted and altered my clothes for me into new styles from old hand-me-downs. I wanted to wear them.

This time Mum was a bit later in getting me up, and I thought I'd try to get up by myself. Swing your legs over the edge of the bed, I thought, which after some trial and error I succeeded in doing.

I was longing to say, "See, Mum, I can do it now," but the moment my feet touched the floor, I felt a jolt right through me. Trying to stand on them, I collapsed miserably. Mum heard the commotion and ran into the room to help me up.

Oh I longed to be better and stronger. This was worse than the measles last year, when I had to stay in complete darkness for fear of going blind; at least then I had something in common with my classmates.

A new word entered my vocabulary – it was **epidemic**. It sounded like a momentous word you should use instead of 'oh dear', or 'goodness gracious me', or even other stop words I had heard, which were frowned upon by adults. So I tried that word – *Epidemic!*

"Epidemic!" I shouted in acceptance of all the medicines I had to swallow. Mum burst out laughing. "That is a big word for a little eight-year-old?"

"So, the doctor says it!" I proffered.

It took almost six weeks for me to get well enough to come downstairs, and not feel so faint and weak.

The first time going down the stairs seemed like a mountain to descend. I had to get my breath back halfway on the landing. Mum said, "Just sit and go down on your bottie!" Oh but my sore bony bum would not let me, so Frans scooped me up halfway for the rest of the stairs and hall, and the long corridor, as well as through the kitchen and into the lounge. I was laid down on Father's long chair, which felt so comfortable. I was grateful to be safe but when I got my broth, I was too tired to eat.

I noticed how thin and sad Mum looked, and Frans even thinner from when I saw him last time with his shirt off. He had biked every day after school to the surrounding villages to ask the farmers for food, to bring home milk and bread etc. for us all simply to stay alive.

After an hour downstairs I was glad to be in bed again, but it was the real start of getting better and stronger. I moved almost without pain after that day, and later went down without help whenever I wanted to, and stay up almost the whole day. But before that day I had a lovely little encounter, with a very small pretty creature.

Whilst looking at a picture book one of the neighbours had brought in, I was startled to hear a sound near me, like *peep, peep, squeak peewit, squeak*. I looked down onto the worn Belgian rug, and there sitting on its hunkers in a teddy bear fashion was the sweetest little mouse. I had seen one before in a picture book and once when I had the measles.

Oh this was great. I had some crumbs left on my plate. I wondered whether to throw these to him, but as soon as I moved he had gone under the bed, scurrying down the plinth, at the side. Oh come back I thought, and he did, after I had thrown the crumbs onto the carpet.

His movements were so quick and squatty. He had almost cleared them, when suddenly the door opened and Mum came in.

"Oh did you drop your plate Mientje?"

"Almost," came the reply. I wanted to tell her, but I'd seen a very nasty little mousetrap in the shed, and I knew what could happen, so I kept it a secret. I wondered if he'd come again, and yes he did every day. I started to leave some small crumbs on purpose for him. It helped me to eat almost everything on my plate, with the prospect of my little friend's daily appearance. It stopped me from being so finicky because of the sheer pleasure of looking forward to this.

I was praised for eating up. Clearing my plate away, Mum said, "You will grow big now that you are better and eating after all." The tremor in Mum's voice was moving, and the cheerful banter and cheeky laughter was evident in my brother and sister's everyday life again. It made me want to eat, sleep and play with Freddy again. Ah where was Freddy? I had heard him but not seen him!

The Girl Who Saw Too Much

Lieve Papa en Rien,   **Dec 1944**

Is it cold where you are? It is freezing here, and I saw lovely star patterns on the glass door to the balcony. They are so pretty; they look like frosty, starry pancakes.

I fall asleep looking at them, especially when the moon shines brightly on them. Mamma says they have come from heaven to make up for the cold, but I am nice and warm in my bed with two warm conies, each with a thick sock on them, so I can't burn myself; but my toes itch so much, it's called chilblains, we all have them.

We had to go to Juliana Hospital to have them treated and bandaged, but they hurt in my special lace up boots.

You have to be careful with your lorry, Dad, on the ice; one lorry here skidded into the canal, and the man was freezing cold when they got him out. They left the lorry in the water; it was too deep.

I would love a pickled herring like we got off the market that time, do you remember that, Papa? We ate them standing up.

I wished you could come home, but at least we got a letter from you, that was wonderful, last week.

       Love you both, from us all, Mientje xxxxxx

Helmi Wolff

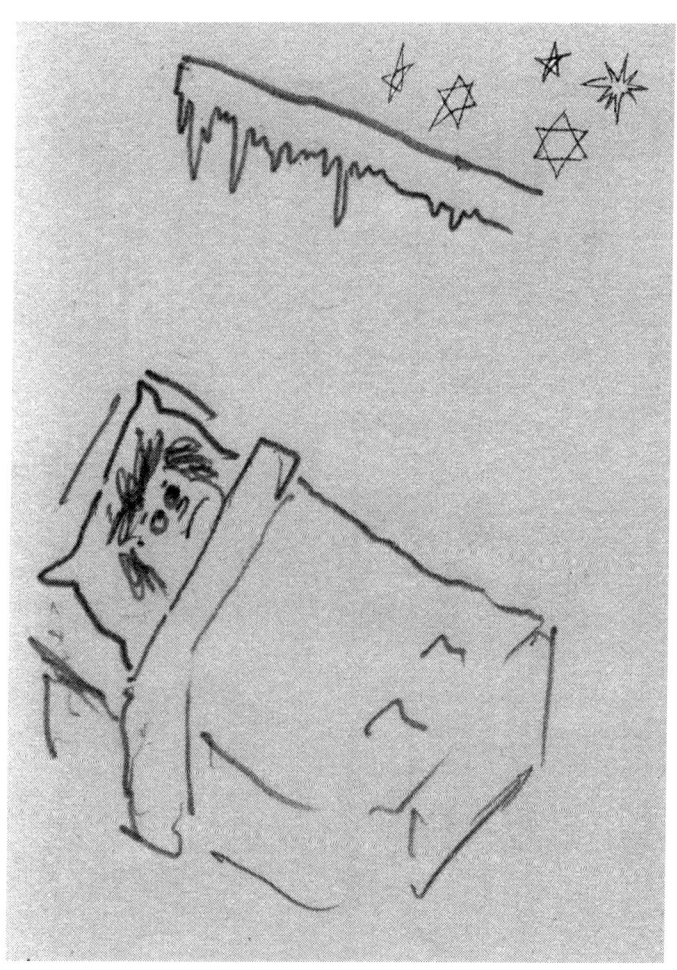

Beautiful Frost Stars.

The Girl Who Saw Too Much

Our Last Six Weeks in the Little Cellar

It was about the size of a small double bed, six steps down from the long corridor under the stairs and next to the indoor loo! The small window had been blocked off with sand bags which I had seen Frans and his friend fill up last week. He also brought home two straw bales from somewhere to further block off the window with.

It was pitch black in there and it was by feel that Mum and I located the two big earthenware stone pots full of runner beans, in some sort of brine, like raw or industrial salt all covered with a round bit of wood like a plate, plus a heavy stone on top of that to keep it all down.

It had been a good year for growing beans and particularly the runners had been plentiful. It was my daily job after school to pick the biggest beans to keep them growing all summer, and after slicing them in small strips, they were added everyday to the already pickled beans in these large barrels. But for now Mum laid two short planks across them to make a table on which she laid a small-embroidered tablecloth. I got quite into the mode of making this space into a sort of dolls home, but for us all, as well!

There was also a shelf incorporated onto the back of the stairs on the other side. That is where all the jars with potted fruit were stored, but a space was made to hold a small oil burner, on which Mum stood a small saucepan with water for a hot drink and of course it also would throw some light.

We lugged the horse-hair mattress from upstairs and laid that on the floor, which exactly fitted wall to wall, plus some blankets and small pillows – it was becoming quite cosy. Next some small plates and cups were put onto the homemade table; also some of that awful black bread with the weirdest low dip in the middle was found, to sustain us through the night.

It looked like a dolly's picnic to me, and in my mind it was all a funny game. "Can I have my dolls in here, Mum?"

"Well not really, only your favourite one then, otherwise there will not be enough space for us all," Ah yes four of us had to sleep in there. Oh what fun I thought, I couldn't wait for it to get dark after supper.

That evening Mum cooked her favourite brown beans, and we still had a few ribs left of our little pig, and fatty pieces which were hung above the range to dry, and to smoke preserve. Mercifully, I did not realise that, because I don't think I could have eaten my pet pig, even though I now did not have to collect food for him anymore. I was just told that he was missing. We all ate well before ascending into the cellar as dusk started to fall.

Hanny came in last, as she had to do her evening creams and exercises before retiring to bed. I had seen her do the stretching ones with which she tried to make her legs longer, also the waist twists and the facial funny ones that made me laugh so much, as she would pull the silliest faces to further make me grin a lot.

"Shove up a bi, Frans," she said.

"If you had been here first you would have got the best spot, Han," he replied, "but as it is, you have to get your ablutions in before eh?"

"You mean, I do my exercises," spouted Han. I again had the vision of her doing these. They were aimed at a thin waist and long legs, and I could not for the life of me understand why she should want long legs and a thin waist, when we were all trying to keep our weight, and cover our legs for the winter. But then she was seventeen and I was told something strange and special happened to you at that age, I couldn't wait to find out when it became my turn.

Frans had homework to do, and so had I. Mum was keen that we should not lag behind with that. I had been given some sums and writing with questions to do, as we now all met in the playground, with the teachers, who would take our completed work to give us new for the next day. The school was still commandeered by German soldiers, who after their barracks were bombed had taken possession of our school, as well as the other schools.

"What is a hay rig?" I asked out of the blue.

"Well you know the one that Wim hides in whenever the raids are on?" proffered Frans. "Well that is one!"

"Oh." Not quite sure what he meant, I looked a bit vacant, and I saw Mum look rather sternly at Frans. He was blushing, and I knew not to ask so many questions now. "I'll do the drawing first," I offered.

But Mum said, "No you can do that when you are tired, but your sums need to be ready for the morning."

Suddenly we heard some hard thuds. Mum looked at us all, to see how we were, and when another much louder bang happened that shook even our cellar, we all looked at each other, but tried not to be alarmed. Mum's free hand was holding on to her little pocket bible.

The bombing went on for much too long a period; every time we thought that it was the end, some more banging and shattering of glass and bricks started – it went on and on. Eventually it did stop mercifully, but we were all a bit on edge, even though I had been cocooned between Mum, Han and Frans to block my ears.

We had to be very quick to go to the toilet next door and it was a major upheaval. If any of us had to go, then we all had to turn over together; everyone had to do the same, to fit in the small cellar. "Keep your feet to yourself, was heard a few times," but Mum said if we finished our homework we would all play housey, housey; she had the game board hidden behind her back against the wall.

"I am winning," I shouted.

"Ah, for the moment," Hanny said. The laughter coming from that crowded cellar was incredible even if a lot of it was due to nerves and relief of penned up fear. Next the most marvellous thing happened, Mum said, "Who would like a cup of hot, chocolate milk?"

Well, need she ask? Where on earth did that come from? Mum sat up to the small shelf with the lighted oil burner, and poured out a cupful of brown liquid for each of us; burned powdered coconut shell from the matting factory mixed with a lick of beet syrup never tasted so marvellous.

It was only much later that I realized how concerned Mum must have been, who without doubt would have had her thoughts with Dad and Rien so far away in the thick of the war's ugly bombing in Germany. And as for us, would we all live to see another day?

The morning came suddenly, as it was now light at about seven o'clock. We ventured out of the cellar, and after our bit of breakfast and a wash, we had to see if all was well, or at least the same as we left it, but it was not.

We saw that two large windows outside on the patio wall had **shattered**, and the shards were hanging down dangerously in sharp peaks. I started to pick some up but was told not to do that. Mum put on her gardening gloves and picked the glass up as best she could. Frans cut his finger, but he insisted that he cleared the ground.

The sun shone in the watery glass making rainbow colours. "Oh could I just have that bit," I asked, but as soon as it was picked up, the rainbow colours disappeared. "Can't we make something with that Frans?" I asked.

The Girl Who Saw Too Much

The bombing of Rotterdam with its huge harbour was horrible as both Mum and Dad had family and friends still living there.

Helmi Wolff

The Liberation

The bombing of the Deventer Bridge
(which was used later to make the film A Bridge too Far,
as the Arnhem Bridge was destroyed).

Frans had gone with his friend Gerard to Deventer, to beg food from the farmers along the canal. Mother knew that the bridge over the river there was a target in the latter days of the war, as the English and Canadians were trying to create havoc for the German army, and vice versa, in our occupied country. Sure enough, on their way back, just as they past the middle of that long bridge, they saw the bomber planes approaching. Moments before they screamed over, Frans and Gerard threw their bikes over the balustrade into the river and then jumped themselves, managing to reach the banks where there was a big factory.

They ducked into the shallow moat as the bombs dropped. The bombs missed the bridge but shattered buildings around. The noise must have been tremendous.

Frans and Gerard held on tightly to each other, covering their faces from the falling rubble, peeping to look at the deafening devastation going on around them. Part of the bridge was damaged but it was not destroyed as they'd dropped their bombs and missed a direct hit.

Huge metal spikes jutted out and shattered concrete hung down into the water in a fog of cement. Debris still flew around them. The huge walls of the building on either side of the bridge were tumbling down. As the two boys ran away over the adjoining field, they saw that the wall against which they had been sheltering was the only thing left standing of that factory. They managed to retrieve one bike.

Mother and I also heard the fighter-bombers approaching. We looked from our flat roof to see in which direction they were going, as they usually flew to Germany to target their strategic points, but they were too low for that. Apeldoorn is only less than an hour's bike ride away from Deventer Bridge and Mum immediately feared the worst. She sank down on her knees and prayed. I also prayed and cried and hoped that Frans and Gerard would be safe. Four agonising hours later Frans, on his bicycle with Gerard on the back, peddled up the road and onto our grit drive. There were floods of tears from us all. We were so thankful they were safe. Frans later told us what had happened and that he had managed to retrieve his bike from the banks after swimming almost to the middle of the canal first. Gerard's was still under the concrete rubble. With most of the transport network now destroyed, we knew that liberation must be soon.

Shortly before our liberation (while we were in our cellar) the local Apeldoorn canal bridge was also bombed. One neighbour in our road had a secret wireless on which he could receive the news of the English and Canadian army coming closer. When we heard that our liberators had stormed Nijmegen, we knew that Arnhem and Oosterbeek would be next. Our liberators, and many others, very dearly paid for the famous onslaught on these towns. Hundreds of graves at Oosterbeek, with white roses among the red poppy fields, tell the story, to be remembered forever.

Closer and closer they pushed until the Rhine was in sight. They were planning to bridge the canal by throwing their mobile bridge to cross it. Our aging doctor who lived close by the canal cautiously received this information. That brave man decided to help, to swim across to tell them the best places. As he did so there were enemy guns trained on him but he lived to tell the tale. Others did not make it.

We received the joyful news of our liberators' arrival whilst still in our cellar that morning, the 5th May 1945. It was Frans who told us. He had been spending the night in a friend's cellar and ran across the road at 5.00 a.m. in the morning to tell us. We all cried with joy and thankfulness.

Mother told Frans not to go out anywhere yet as there was crossfire and fighting in the streets of Apeldoorn, so Frans stayed with us. We didn't stay down in the cellar but got out into the house and began to eat and drink.

At 8.00 a.m. Hanny said, "I'm going to look." So together with Frans she did, reporting back that people were streaming out of their houses and that they saw the German soldiers being rounded up and marched to the border of Germany. Some of them had picked up bikes and were peddling hell for leather back home to their own country. Were they glad it was all over too? I expect they were. After all, they had also had heavy losses. Everyone wanted them to go: good riddance to them.

Mother and I left home by 9.00 a.m. but not before she had found white dresses for herself and me. We wore orange sashes across our shoulders and over our hips. Where had she been able to hide these? It showed her firm belief that we would have cause to wear them later.

I felt the tremendous excitement and relief of everyone and as we got to Asselsestraat, leading to the Hoofdweg of the village centre, joyous people were lining the pavements, waving and singing, shouting in the happy knowledge that at last we would be free. Then we saw the first heavily armoured tanks looming enormously, victorious in triumph, advancing along our sandy roads. English and Canadian soldiers beamed down at us. They were throwing pure white slices of bread (I have a photo of this) but we didn't even recognise it as bread, having never seen this kind of food before – *Manna from Heaven* we called it.

Girls of fifteen years and older were hoisted on board and rode along with our liberators, while chocolate pieces and chewing gum and cigarettes were thrown out at us. The men grappled for the cigarettes while we children gathered up the sweets. I did not know what chocolate was, much less chewing gum, which I learnt to like a lot later.

We yelled and screamed, **"Thank you, thank you."** It went on all day until I was so tired that Mother had to invent a skipping game to help me put mind over matter to get home. I suddenly saw my beautiful, seventeen-year-old sister, Hanny, on top of a tank. She saw me and yelled, "Come on, come on," but Mamma showed me how to eat that incredibly white bread instead. Frans ran round in a delirium of joy with friends.

Helmi Wolff

Nightmares

One reoccurring nightmare was utterly devastating.
"Stand still, child," someone boomed into my ear.
"I will, I will," but I knew I couldn't.
A face with glazed eyes came up, right in front of my face. It started to distort and the damp lips moved. Words slithered in and out of that wet mouth, a doughy tongue wriggling inside, sucking in and out.
Mesmerized I stood, and then ran and ran, but my left foot tripped me up, and he caught me, making slurpy soggy sounds, spittle running down his saggy chin as if he was going to eat me.
"Mientje, Mientje," called Mum, while she shook me gently.
"Oh, oh," I cried. "He tried to eat me, Mum."
"No, love, just cuddle up with me now."
It took some time for my crying to stop, but somehow this nightmare and others often repeated themselves, especially when I was ill.
One that plagued me often was, "Do you understand child?"
"Yes, Miss, I do," but in truth I hadn't a clue, and I was terrified of her.
She showed me up; if I was daydreaming, and made me stand in front of the class, sometimes with a tall dunce's cap on, which she had me make first, of any old smelly paper while the other kids sniggered at my fumbling efforts.
One day she got a much younger but very bright little girl to compete with me standing and writing on the blackboard. "Now," she said, "spell advantageous, and incredible," and other quite

advanced words. I spelt it wrong of course, but the clever little girl got it right. Often it ended in my being punished by three strokes of the ruler over my hand. This was very much based on reality but the dream made it so intense and horrifying.

Sometimes I had amazing dreams, when the moon shone full into my bedroom window, casting strange shadows, all round the room.

Sleep overtook me, and I drifted into an amazing grotto, with shiny, tall creatures.

One bent down to look at me, than beckoned for me to follow. Suddenly others jumped down and I felt as if I was choking, but it didn't last.

A more frightening one was always connected with the *horrible soldiers*, carrying long guns with bayonets and sticking them in people.

If it was damp weather, I could hear the shrill whistle of the steam trains, which I hated and always tried to put the pillow over my head to exclude that sound.

My screaming sent Mum running up, to calm me down again.

After I had sore eyes with conjunctivitis, Mum managed to get some cow's saliva from a farm, which was renowned for curing bad eyes.

Well it was just as well that I didn't know, but it really did the trick.

Later I overheard her speaking about this great remedy, and I again had great slobbering nightmares about that. "Well," asked Mum, "surely you are glad your eyes are now better?" What a silly girl, I felt.

Even knitting that stupid cotton towel was a bit of a silly nightmare; the fact was that I just didn't see that knitting was as useful as reading or drawing.

But my most feared one was, falling, falling, and falling ever deeper in this dark pit, screaming and struggling hardly able to breathe. Not being able to stop until the slimy green water had closed over me and I was struggling for breath, by which time Mum would be trying to shake me awake saying soothing words.

Not all dreams were nightmares; in fact the happy dreams probably were as many.

These were usually about our family and musical evenings, where all of a sudden I was able to play the old zither, like a harp, or sing like an angel or even play the piano with great gusto. Oh wow!

The Dug Out

I was told a true story, later by Rien, (set in Düsseldorf Germany where Rien and Dad were during most of the war time, used as forced labour).

Where was the tower? Where was everything – the little clock tower on top of the hospital that was such a familiar landmark? All he could see was a blaze of flames, smoke rising from bombed buildings, rubble and dense brick dust everywhere, sirens bellowing above the din, drowning every other sound that must be there. Oh God what a hell!

Standing on top of a burned and half fallen wall, he stood breathless. Gasping, looking over the smoking rooftops. The air raid over; it was followed by the immediate chaos and danger of the still falling buildings and dense thick smoke, like a stifling fog hanging over it all.

Rien had torn both hands getting this far, but he'd hardly noticed that, all he could think of is, 'where is Dad?' It thundered in his head. Not knowing in which direction to go, he began to run again towards where he had last seen the hospital.

The town was unrecognisable. It didn't even look like a town any more, more like a mass hell grave. He heard cries and shouts for help and he tried to lift a huge lintel which lay half across a woman who screamed that her children were buried under the rubble inside. She was freed and a dog sprang out from below. "I have to find my father," he shouted back.

Half jumping and grappling with some iron railings he managed to get down again, and just did not stop running, running eastwards.

It had got to be east of the railway station. Oh the agony of not knowing and people crying and wailing. He tried to help, his heart pounding in his ears and chest, running again to where the hospital had stood.

The worst fear gripped his throat as he ran round the last bend. The hospital should now be in sight.

Oh please God, for a moment he stood nailed to the ground; there was only some left of it, and the wing where Dad had been was demolished. He tried to get near to see. Other men and women tried to do the same. "They are down there," someone said. "The huge shelter under the building must still be there. We'll need everyone and everything to get inside."

Large machinery started to arrive, but Rien could not wait for that. He started to move the broken stones with his torn hands. 'Dad has got to be down there in that cellar,' he thought, 'he would only just have had his operation.' Dread gripped his throat again.

"Get out of there," someone shouted.

"My dad," he shouted back.

"No move, you'll not do it like that lad, we'll bore a tunnel. Everything will collapse on itself otherwise." Horrified he jumped aside, tears streaming down, oh God, I pray, please, please help us.

The huge machine got closer and closer, and then it seemed an arm came out from it, with a drill. With a dreadful noise the drill started turning fast. Terrified everyone watched, while part of the towering and lunging hospital wall shuddered overhead.

He was one of the crowd now, while he realized that all these people were in the same state as him. Most of them had a loved one in that hospital, and only a few of these would have been transferred to the shelter. How could Dad have got there from the operating table? Would they have had time?

The noise of the drill overpowered everything else, a dread hush hung over the crowd. Could they get through, and if they did, would they be able to reach them, even if they were still alive? Would their loved ones be amongst the survivors?

The agony of waiting. Suddenly a shout went up, **"Stop, stop."** They had been drilling in the wrong place. A second shaft was drilled, 'Oh pray, let them find the right spot.'

Rien's mind went back a long way, to when he and Dad had built that big bonfire. How high it was. He could see it so clearly now, and Dad had to lift him to put the last bits of wood on the top. Later in the glowing cinders, they had found the warped remains of Frankie's little lorry, which must have been hidden on the ground before they started. But that always stayed a secret; he'd cleared that away with the rest, in case he'd find it. For weeks Frankie had been looking for his lorry, and neither Dad nor Rien had the heart to tell him of its charred remains.

Then there was the day they'd spent fishing, and Dad had caught a whopper. It all but got to the local paper under 'fishing times'. For weeks the lads at school discussed it, till Rien got sick of it, especially since he himself had not actually caught anything worth mentioning that season, and it wasn't as if they ate them for tea like Aunty Nora always suggested. As Dad usually let them go again, so there was nothing to show for it.

Not all of it had been a free and easygoing childhood, growing up had its problems. He hated it when people used to say, "Oh your voice has broken now, what a lovely deep sound." There was the time Aunty Hilda came round after a long absence. She looked him up and down and said, "My, my, he is really getting like his father now, he even sounds like him."

That's when he noticed how enormous she was, and remarked that it was a good job he didn't take after her then. But then realizing that he had been a bit quick off the mark, spun on his heals to race up the stairs, under protests from Mother, whilst apologizing to Aunt Hilda.

Someone gave him a poke in the ribs, and shouted, "Hey dozy, wake up will yer? Don't just stand there; move yourself, this is where we're drilling. Come on shift." With a great jerk he sprang aside, what was the matter with him? The air raid; Dad, oh, this is reality, here and now, the bombing; everything rushed into his head again he felt like it was exploding. His head was thumping and swimming, with the ache inside.

Again the machine moved close and started drilling furiously. Some of the crowd had gone. A small boy had wandered off and started playing in the rubble, while his mother ran to get him, and then pressed him close to her.

A sob came from another woman standing pale and shaken. All the available men were helping.

Rien wanted to help too, furiously, but the machine was much more powerful and it was drilling with the most deafening noise. Stones and pieces of wall were still crashing down here and there. Suddenly he was back in the great woods with his dog Skip, and Dad was calling him.

He had wandered off, and by the time he'd heard his call, they'd been searching for him for half an hour, in the half dark damp mist. He hadn't even missed them, and it was not until he was much older, that he realised what a turn he'd given his parents.

Skippy and he were as one, inseparable. Where he went Skippy went too, and it was a daily agony to leave Skip behind when he went to school. He'd go anywhere with him, 'safe as houses', so long as Skip was there.

It was certainly awful when he had to be in hospital for weeks with a bad head injury, which had a lot of after effects. He worried about Skip more than the injuries he had sustained.

Suddenly the drilling stopped; it jolted Rien out of his daydreaming. An excited hush went through the crowd. One of the men had gone down the shaft and everyone came forward. A head came up, it was an unconscious man, he looked dreadful. Rien's heart gave a jolt and a woman started crying, she all but collapsed.

Oh please God, let it be Dad, still alive down there. A second man came up, and an agonized groan escaped a man's throat, it was his son. Several more emerged to see the daylight supported and tied with ropes, some of them looking more dead than alive.

So moved to tears was Rien by all that he was witnessing, that when suddenly a grey head appeared at the surface, he just looked at him; then a smile of recognition spread between them. Rien rushed forward. "Dad," is all he could manage as the tears streamed over both their faces.

Helmi Wolff

Homecoming

I can hear a lot of shouting; we all heard quite a lot of joyous upheaval. Running outside to hear what could be the cause, we saw our neighbours running towards us, shouting, **"He has been seen**, we've spotted Wolff and Rien at the top of the road."

"What?" we all exclaimed, "what do you mean?"

"Yer Dad and brother coming home, love. Oh, Mrs Wolff, he's coming home dear, we've seen him!"

Mum stood almost dazed and tears streaming down her face, uttered, **"Oh thank you, Lord, thank you**, thank you." She just couldn't move and almost sank to her knees in exhausted thankfulness.

I started running up the road, in jubilation. Frans overtook me, shouting at me, "He's coming home; he's here oh, oh." I was running blindly with just one thought, 'Daddy and Rien, Daddy and Rien'.

Then we saw them turning the bend in the road, **oh Daddy, Daddy**. They were pushing a little cart with stuff tied onto it, but they just left it standing in the road and exhausted, limped and ran to us.

Faces wet with tears and hugs, hugs, hugs, hugs. "Mien, Mien," he said. "You have grown, Mien." He scooped me up. Frans and Rien were hugging never to let go, we all ran to Mum and Hanny, who was holding Mum up in front of our house and then… Dad held Mum in his strong arms, Rien, Frans, Han and I all held onto them as well, laughing, crying, hugging. Ohhh! And that's how we walked into our house together.

The Girl Who Saw Too Much

Who was the first one to speak? I don't know, but, "How are you, Dad and Rien? Oh how great to see you. We have waited and dreamed of this for so long," and would you believe it, the usual or unusual rumpus of dancing round the big table, happened again, singing, "He's home, they're home, home, home, we are together, they're home!"

Suddenly, neighbours thronged at the door and were also moved to tears, to see us so utterly happy. And where is the little iron wheeled cart they walked with all the way from Germany? Our neighbour brought it along. "Oh good, good, thank you, well what is in it and on it?"

We all sat down, with cups of tea Mum made of her minced roasted coconut shells, which tasted remarkably good, for all, and the stories abounded. So many questions, but that could wait; Dad and Rien were exhausted, needing to rest desperately. Dad sat in his old long chair; I could hardly believe it! He said that he learned to grow tobacco. Well now I really thought that had to be a tall story, so we all laughed and they laughed with us.

Helmi Wolff

Papa, in front of our house, after the war.

The Girl Who Saw Too Much

Analogue, On the 60th Anniversary – Commemoration of the Ill Fated

'Market Garden Operation', (Parachute Drop of Our Liberators) in Oosterbeek, near Arnhem, and Apeldoorn.

On September 17, 2004, I was privileged and felt thrilled but emotional, to attend the commemoration of the ill fated Para drop, in which so many English, Canadian, Polish, Turkish and even more nationalities, courageous paratroopers lost their lives, and so many were injured and maimed.

The cemetery was packed, many old paratroopers present, proudly wearing their plum coloured berets. Officials were at the front near the cenotaph. I was able to see, as there were stepped platforms for the people at the back to stand on.

The Dutch national anthem was played; everyone stood and sang.

Soldiers and other official persons saluted the dead. All offered their silent respects for the fallen heroes.

Queen Beatrix stepped forward to lay a wreath at the memorial. Then Prince Charles also honoured the dead to lay a wreath, at the foot of the 'nameless soldier' grave, and at the memorial.

Many dignitaries followed suit, while a tear glistened on many faces, of those who witnessed this solemn event.

Having witnessed the actual drop, as I had, with my brother Frans, on September 17, 1944, and seeing also that they were shot at in the air, I felt again like the little girl who saw it all, overcome with emotion, at the memories of this black day.

When the ceremony was over, almost everyone went to look at the long lines of white gravestones, many identifying the particular gravestone of their families. A father or son, an uncle, a brother or nephew was remembered and honoured with so much respect and gratitude.

One old soldier, came up to me, and said he had come to see four of his old friends who had jumped at the same time as himself, but he was the only survivor. I was moved to tears, and all I could utter was, "Oh thank you so much for liberating us, thank you, thank you." I do remember his face and his name.

The Girl Who Saw Too Much

At the Oosterbeek Remembrance Garden on
the 60th anniversary of the Market Garden Drop
"Are you the little girl who saw it all?"
"Yes. Oh thank you for liberating us."

Helmi Wolff

The Bronze of Queen Juliana on her bicycle at Veluwe, thoughtfully being admired, as she passed our house so often.

The Girl Who Saw Too Much

Mum's Mum, Grandma Nieuwstraten.

Helmi Wolff

Dad's Mum, Grandma Wolff.

The Girl Who Saw Too Much

Great Grandma Homberg, Mum's gran.